"Lean thinking is helping make governments more effective, more efficient and more accountable to the people we serve. *Delivering Results That Matter* showcases key Lean principles and offers case studies about how they're being used. It makes a strong case for the power of Lean to transform our organizations and drive continuous improvement."

–Jay Inslee,
Governor of Washington

"From the outset of our operational excellence initiative, the goal was to instill Lean thinking within the organization versus pursuing formal accreditation as a "lean" organization. This aligned with our cultural change initiative, which is focused on instilling, within our leadership and our team, a low-cost, customer-focused, operationally excellent company. Adopting the practices outlined in *Delivering Results that Matter* has transitioned us to that end in a significant and sustainable manner. Leaders and staff are developing a mind-set of identifying and removing waste. We have moved from improvement being a project or a special event to part of our way of managing the business and delivering services to our customers. Our Lean management system encourages our leaders to have a different perspective on their role; moving away from being the "chief problem solver" to empowering employee teams of problem solvers. The discipline we are building will continue to sustain and build on our improvements in customer service, efficiency, and employee engagement."

– Mark Blucher, President and CEO,
Insurance Corporation of British Columbia

"Lean Management is a powerful strategy to create mindsets and behaviors that allow public sector organizations to promote and sustain continuous improvement. Chagani and Whitehead provide a clear roadmap for organizations to embark on their own Lean journey to become more efficient, effective, and accountable to the public."

– Mike Harris,
Partner and Board Chair, PwC Canada

A POST HILL PRESS BOOK

Delivering Results That Matter:
Transforming Public Services Through Lean Management
© 2018 by Haneef Chagani and Shelley Whitehead
All Rights Reserved

No part of this book may be reproduced, stored in a retrieval system, or transmitted by any means without the written permission of the author and publisher.

Post Hill Press
New York • Nashville
posthillpress.com

Published in the United States of America

DELIVERING RESULTS THAT MATTER

TRANSFORMING PUBLIC SERVICES
THROUGH LEAN MANAGEMENT

Haneef Chagani & Shelley Whitehead

Table of Contents

Advance Praise for *Delivering Results that Matter* i
Acknowledgments xi
Foreword xiii
Introduction xvii

Chapter 1: The Lean Advantage 1
    Global Public Sector Lean Implementation 1
    What Is Lean? 2
    Why Lean? 3
    What Lean Isn't 3
    Lean Principles and Waste 4
    Lean Methods 6
        Value Stream Mapping (VSM) Events 6
        Rapid Process Improvement Workshops (RPI)/Kaizen Events 7
        Mistake Proofing 8
        Six Sigma 9
        5S 11
        3P 13
        A3 15
        Visual Controls 15
        Strategy Deployment/Hoshin Kanri 15
        Lean Management 17

Chapter 2: The Customer and Citizen 19
    Who Is the Customer? 19
    Voice of the Customer 21
    The Customer at the Center? 22

Engaging the Citizen 23
Chapter 3: The Lean Journey 30
    Phase 1: Strategy and Assessment 31
    Phase 2: Mobilization 33
    Phase 3: Initiation 35
    Phase 4: Integration 37
    Phase 5: Sustainment 37
    Deployment Trajectories 38

Chapter 4: Governance and Oversight 45
    Leadership 46
    Governance 46
        Lean Steering Committee 47
        Lean Office 47
        Lean Deployment Champions 47
        Lean Leaders 48
    Engaging the Board and Elected Representatives 48
    "Push" versus "Pull" Participation 53
    Training 53
    Resource Allocation 54
    Enterprise Lean Forums 54
    Measuring Results 55
    Public Sector Lean Accountability 60
    Measuring Lean Implementation 60
    Reporting Progress and Communicating Results 61

Chapter 5: Leading, Managing, and Strategic Use of Lean 66
    What Is Lean Management? 66
    Principal Elements of Lean Management 67
        Leader Standard Work 68
        Visual Controls 69
        Daily Accountability/Management 70
        Leadership Discipline 71
        Problem Solving 72
        Leadership Behaviors 72

  Lean Management System..74
  Strategic Use of Lean...82
    Value Stream Identification and Selection................83
    Using Lean Thinking to Address Complex Issues......83
  Lean Maturity Assessment..90

Chapter 6: Lean Strategic Planning and Deployment.......... 94
  The Process..95
  The Visibility Wall..95
  The Wall Walk..98

Chapter 7: Nudging with Lean...103
  The "What" and "Why" of Nudge...............................103
  Lean Methods and Nudge Practices..............................106
    Libertarian Paternalism, Choice Architecture, and Lean.......106
    Lean Is a Nudge..107
    Nudging with Lean...108

Chapter 8: Integrating Lean Management with
Public Sector Digital Transformation 112
  Integration of Lean Management 113

Conclusion 119
Bibliography..121
About the Authors.. 125
Index... 127

List of Case Studies

Oil and Gas Technical Application 7
A Canadian Medical Laboratory 8
Mistake Proofing in a Hospital 9
Claims Front End Process Improvement
    Workplace Injury Claims Processing 10
5S in a Canadian Highways Ministry 12
New Canadian Regional Hospital 14
Using *Hoshin Kanri* Across Saskatchewan's Education Sector 16
Washington State Correctional Industries 25
The United States National Institutes of Health (NIH)
    Lean Journey 40
Government of Saskatchewan, Canada 50
Washington State Department of Corrections 57
A Canadian Province's Ministry of Transportation 64
Insurance Corporation of British Columbia (ICBC), Canada 76
Lower Mainland Facilities Management (LMFM),
    British Columbia, Canada 81
Results Washington 85
Export Development Canada (EDC) 90
Using Lean Strategic Planning and Deployment (*Hoshin Kanri*)
    Across Saskatchewan's Healthcare System 100
Visual Management and Productivity,
    British Columbia Crown Corporation 108
The City of Denver, Colorado 109
Financial Services Organization 117

Acknowledgments

This book would not have been possible without the assistance and support of so many people.

We begin by thanking Governor Jay Inslee for motivating us all in the foreword, and Rich Roesler and Pam Pannkuk for hosting our visits to Washington State to learn about "Results Washington." Thanks also to Jody Becker-Green, Bryan Irwin, Andi May, Jeannie Miller, and Jim Nelson from the Department of Corrections for their assistance and especially for the visit to Stafford Creek Corrections Center. Thanks to Doug Moen, Kent Campbell, Max Hendricks, Dan Florizone, Don Wincherauk, Pauline Rousseau, Gord Tweed, Jocelyn Robinson, Mark Anderson, Trish Livingstone, Lori Evert, and all the Saskatchewan Lean Leaders and Deployment Champions who contributed information and stories on Saskatchewan's Lean journey. Thanks to Brian Goodger from the U.S. National Institutes of Health (USNIH) and Chelsea Bridge, Chris Houchin, and Jill Olmstead from PwC US who connected us with the USNIH story. The Lower Mainland Facilities Management case study was made possible by Paul Becker, Ian Clearie, Rian Dodds, and Toven Simonsen. Thanks also to Kathy Parslow, Barbara Meens Thistle, and Ron Matthews for their support for the Insurance Corporation of British Columbia case study. The Export Development Canada (EDC) case study was informed by the enthusiasm and assistance of Scott Powell, and thanks to Craig Szelestowski for his story of Lean in a provincial Ministry of Transportation. As well, Brian Elms and J.B. Wogan from the City of Denver, thanks to you for your contribution regarding the City of Denver's combined use of Lean and Nudge.

We also want to thank PwC for their support and encouragement. In particular, we thank Jie Feng, Steven Williams, Tyler Totman, Vanessa

Harrison-Chambers, Susan McIntyre, Robert Mah Ming, Steven Burgermeister, Tom Ehwalt, Julia Heskel, Denise Lee, John Moore, Bianca Salentyn, Melaina Vinski, James McLean, Adam Crutchfield, and Mike Harris for the assistance they have provided over the past few years.

Thanks, too, for the invaluable contribution of our editor, Debra Englander. Her patience, persistence, and helpful suggestions made the book so much clearer and suitable for a global audience. Likewise, thanks to Post Hill Press for publishing and promoting the book.

Finally, we owe our deepest thanks to our families. Shelley thanks Rick August for his quiet encouragement, patience, and support, as well as sons Sean, Adam, and Kevin Hoover, and mother Renee Whitehead. Haneef thanks Parinda and sons Hafiz and Khalil for their ongoing support, encouragement and love.

Foreword

Jay Inslee, Governor of Washington

Innovation is no longer an option. It's an expectation. It's shaping how we work, learn, shop, communicate, and travel. Customers expect speed, intuitive interactions, and responsiveness.

Those same expectations increasingly apply to government. People who are used to shopping, banking, texting and getting real-time answers to virtually anything on their mobile devices are not likely to have a lot of patience for slow replies, paper forms, and archaic processes.

People expect better. They deserve better.

I first saw Lean at work as a congressman from Washington state. *I was able to learn how Lean thinking was engaging employees and improving efficiency and quality at places like the Boeing Company and Virginia Mason Medical Center.* Lean has helped Boeing produce more aircraft in smaller workspaces. At Virginia Mason, it has revolutionized patient care. And in both places – and dozens more Washington employers – it has engaged employees in problem solving to improve quality for customers.

As governor, I've championed Lean thinking across our workforce and seen the results. Tens of thousands of our employees have been exposed to Lean principles. In the first three years alone, agencies reported three thousand Lean improvement efforts. We've slashed backlogs, simplified forms, cut errors, saved millions of dollars, and improved quality. Our two thousand-person annual Lean government conference is the biggest of its kind in the world.

In the process, we've empowered and engaged those closest to the work: our frontline staff. They interact with customers. They see the glitches in the forms and processes. They see what's valuable and what's not. By drawing on that experience to help craft solutions, we serve customers better, streamline the work and empower employees to continuously improve. Some of our biggest evangelists for Lean are line staff who've seen the changes in their own work. I see this myself when I visit agencies unannounced and talk with staff. Their pride and enthusiasm is palpable, because they've seen the results they have achieved.

We're also using Lean principles on some of the biggest challenges my state faces. Things like public health, education, homelessness, and recidivism. Through my Results Washington team, we're using Lean principles in data-driven, collaborative work to find what works and build on that. In a very real way, Lean is helping us learn our way forward.

Along the way, *we've learned some lessons*:

- **Create a safe climate for people to bring problems forward.** We can't fix what we don't know about. Encourage a climate in which all employees – no matter where they are in the organizational chart – aren't afraid to point out a problem.
- **Focus on outcomes, not outputs.** It's tempting to try to measure success in terms of how many people have been trained or certified. But stay focused on the why: We're doing this to get real results that matter to the people we serve.
- **Embrace and celebrate early adopters.** Organizational transformation is hard in any large organization, so cultivate those who are willing to jump in and try a new thing. Tell their stories. Celebrate their successes. Even if they fail – because that's inevitable in a culture of experimentation and innovation – focus on what they've learned and how they'll move ahead.
- **Don't be afraid to ask for help.** In Washington, we're fortunate to have a vast number of organizations that have been using Lean principles for years. We reached out to them and asked them to loan us their expertise to help our workforce learn more about Lean. Some hosted seminars for hundreds of state workers. Others facilitated improvement efforts. Some coached teams or consulted by phone. None of it cost us anything, and it gave our effort a huge jump-start early on.
- **Meet people where they are.** Lean terms – kaizen, 5S, Kanban boards, and such – can be intimidating. We often joke that we

use "stealth Lean" – encouraging the principles without necessarily calling out some of the terminology.
- **Work with supervisors and managers.** In many cases, these are people who've built up systems that work for them over many years. They're concerned – rightfully – about accountability. Work with them to manage any anxiety and develop team-coaching skills.
- **Avoid the temptation to measure success purely in dollars.** There's often a tendency to pigeonhole Lean largely as a cost-savings tool. It's much broader than that. It's about improving quality, focusing on value to customers and streamlining work. In our case, we've seen many examples of how Lean is helping us manage growing workloads with the same resources. But keep expectations in check: Although savings are likely to result, Lean is a long-term quality improvement philosophy.
- **Avoid a one-size-fits-all mind-set.** Although we standardized basic principles and oversight, we deliberately allowed agencies flexibility in their Lean journey. It's a reality that organizational cultures are different. We also wanted to allow agencies to be miniature labs in finding which approaches worked best, and to learn from each other.

None of this is easy. Some of it's really hard. But quality matters just as much in government as it does in the private sector – sometimes even more. We protect the vulnerable, serve the sick and do the work that no one else can do. It is a noble calling, and in Washington state we've seen for ourselves how Lean helps us do this important work even better.

Introduction

Globalization, economic pressures, demographic changes, technological advancements, and the rise of social media are putting increased pressure on governments around the world to renew and revitalize public services to ensure long-term sustainability. While public expectations that governments will be accessible and responsive are increasing, budgets are stretched with governments strained in their ability to manage, especially in light of increasing infrastructure costs. Among the many issues faced by governments at all levels are the maintenance of roads and schools, aging water and sewer infrastructure, inadequate transportation systems, the management of public safety, environmental challenges, and the ever increasing costs of education, healthcare, and the military.

Now, more than ever, individuals are calling for public services – those provided directly by governments, by crown corporations, or by third party delivery agents such as health authorities and school divisions – to be effective, efficient, and responsive to what citizens want and need. Many governments around the world are responding by refreshing and renewing public services to ensure they are relevant for the future.

We believe Lean management is key to public service reform because it can help governments tackle complex problems while increasing transparency, demonstrating accountability, and doing more with less. Sometimes misunderstood as simply being about process improvement, Lean is actually a business philosophy, leadership, and management approach. It focuses on improving transactional processes to deliver improvement at the operational level as well as transformational change in strategy, management, and culture to achieve and sustain maximum performance across the organization. By implementing Lean, governments can improve programs, services, and processes, making them better, safer, and more efficient and citizens can receive the quality services they need and expect. Thoughtful implementation of Lean management principles in public-sector workplaces results in an environment of continuous improvement, problem solving, accountability, and measurement.

Implementing Lean across the public sector can be a vital mechanism for governments to solicit fresh ideas which challenge the status quo and lead to innovation. It can also help governments work horizontally, across departments, to address and manage issues that span multiple ministries, departments, or agencies. Savings achieved through increased efficiency can then be retargeted to other strategic priorities. Lean adds value for the customers who use public services, the employees who provide those services, and the taxpayers who pay for them.

Public sector Lean implementation is in the public interest because it ensures better outcomes for dollars spent. It can help government deliver on public expectations – namely, revitalized public services that deliver results – as illustrated below:

Driver Diagram for Refreshing Public Services

Refreshed, Renewed & Revitalized Public Services that Deliver Results (Economy, Health, Environment, Education, Justice, Public Safety, Social Services)

- Improved Service
- Increased Efficiency
- Enhanced Safety
- Improved Governance

- Productive Workforce
- Better Measurement
- Strengthened Accountability
- Enhanced Transparency

LEAN

A Pragmatic, Disciplined Approach

This book is written for committed public servants in all levels of governments around the world – national or federal; provincial or state; and municipal or local. It is written for leaders, managers, and supervisors in departments, ministries, branches, and crown corporations. It is also for anyone responsible for the direct delivery of important public services such as those in the health, education, and post-secondary sectors including colleges, universities, and technical schools.

Lean is a pragmatic, yet disciplined approach to achieving operational excellence. This book provides practical advice about how it can be implemented effectively within public-sector organizations to improve the quality, efficiency, and safety of programs and services. A variety of case studies are provided to illustrate concepts, as well as the use of Lean by federal, state, provincial, and municipal jurisdictions across Canada and the U.S. By using Lean, governments can increase the effectiveness of public services. It is the ideal approach for delivering results that matter to citizens.

Chapter 1 provides an overview of public sector Lean implementation around the world. It then goes on to describe what Lean is and how it can be used for the improvement of public-sector programs and services. A variety of Lean methods are highlighted, along with relevant case studies.

Seeing programs and services through the eyes of the customer and designing improvement accordingly are the focus of Chapter 2. Lean is intended, in part, to engage citizens directly to improve the public services which they, as the consumers of those services, utilize. A case study from the Washington State Department of Corrections illustrates how inmates are being engaged and trained in Lean as part of developing marketable job skills and instilling and promoting a positive work ethic, as well as reducing the tax burden of the correctional system.

Chapter 3 provides an overview of the public-sector journey. As organizations implement Lean they can expect to go through five distinct phases: assessment, mobilization, initiation, integration, and sustainment. Each phase is explained and a Lean journey case study is presented from the National Institutes of Health in the United States.

Governance and oversight is the focus of Chapter 4, which provides practical advice for managers implementing Lean in a public-sector environment. Three case studies are provided: the first is from the Government of Saskatchewan, where Lean is being used in all government ministries and across the health and education sectors; the second is from Washington State Department of Corrections illustrating how Lean is being used to ensure the priorities and direction of the elected are implemented from executive management, to middle management, to frontline employees, and to inmates; and the third is a description by Craig Szelestowski, President and Founder of Lean Agility's Lean Government Practice, of how use of Lean by a Canadian province's Ministry of Transportation significantly reduced backlogs without requiring an investment in technology or employee headcount.

Leadership, Lean management (which focuses on equipping frontline supervisors, managers, and executive leaders with the skills and tools they need to mange effectively and foster a culture of continuous improvement), and strategic use of Lean are the focus of Chapter 5. The chapter includes case studies from the Insurance Corporation of British Columbia which has launched its "Operational Excellence" program based on Lean thinking; Results Washington, the State's performance management initiative which drives the operations of government through use of Lean at both a strategic and tactical level; and Export Development Canada's (EDC) transformational program which shows the role an external maturity assessment conducted by the Shingo Institute played in helping EDC take the next steps in its Lean journey.

Chapter 6 is about strategic planning and deployment and illustrates the use of *Hoshin Kanri* (a Japanese phrase meaning management of the strategic direction setting process) to develop and link an organization's strategic plan with a disciplined process to ensure the plan is implemented, adapted, and improved over time. A case study from the Province of Saskatchewan shows how Lean strategic deployment is being used to unite all health regions in the province, along with the provincial government, to support a common set of strategic priorities.

Combining use of Lean with "Nudge" theory is the focus of Chapter 7. When used together there is significant potential for public services to be refreshed and renewed to achieve improved outcomes for the public. Nudge theory advocates helping people to make rational decisions, rather than relying on cognitive biases. Its origins in behavioral economics are described and case examples are presented to illustrate "Nudging with Lean."

Finally, Brian Elms and J.B. Wogan from the City of Denver provide an overview of how they are using Nudge and Lean in a disciplined way to achieve improved municipal services.

Chapter 8 speaks to the benefits of integrating the Lean Management philosophy in organizations' digital transformation journey. Unfortunately, improving business processes is often seen as a separate activity from technology implementation. We will show how Lean Management, customer experience, and technology implementation can be used together as an overall transformation methodology benefiting organizations in many ways including delivering increased value to customers, reducing time to deliver digital services, realizing early cost savings and capacity gains and, most importantly, changing the way people think, feel, and behave in the workplace. A case study from a public sector Canadian financial services organization is presented to illustrate the approach.

This book is a practical guide to transforming public services through Lean Management. It demonstrates how national, state, provincial, and municipal governments are using Lean to lead, manage, and improve public services. The governments we profile are public sector Lean leaders and we can learn a great deal from them. They know that Lean is about much more than process improvement and, in fact, that Lean Management can be used strategically to achieve results. As authors, it is our hope that this book inspires you to embark on your own Lean journey.

Chapter 1

THE LEAN ADVANTAGE

Global Public Sector Lean Implementation

Numerous governments and public-sector organizations around the world are embracing Lean. Some are doing it on a project by project basis within government branches, departments, or ministries while others are using it across the entire public service sector, with outside vendors and with major third-party delivery agencies funded by government such as school divisions, health providers, colleges, and universities.

In Canada, four provinces are using Lean extensively: Saskatchewan implemented Lean government-wide in 2010, New Brunswick in 2011, British Columbia in 2012, and Manitoba in 2013. The Government of Saskatchewan's major third parties are also using Lean, including all regional health authorities, select school divisions, and select post-secondary institutions. In 2014, the Government of Canada announced its intention to use Lean more extensively as part of implementing its Blueprint 2020 vision for transforming the public service. The cities of Thunder Bay and Kingston in Ontario and Abbotsford in British Columbia are also using Lean.

More than half of the states in the U.S. are using Lean, to some extent, with Minnesota (2008), Iowa (2009), Colorado (2011), Connecticut (2011), Ohio (2011), Tennessee (2011), Washington (2011), Arizona (2012), Wisconsin (2012), and Rhode Island (2015) having the most advanced implementation. These state websites indicate they have taken an enterprise approach to implementing Lean; they are using it in all departments across the state government.

Lean is also being used by the UK Government and in the Scottish public sector. It is transforming healthcare in Brazil and China, and education in Norway. The cities of Amersfoort in the Netherlands and Melbourne in Australia are active proponents of Lean. Increasingly, it is the norm rather than the exception for jurisdictions to use Lean, at least to some extent, to improve the delivery of public services.

Lean thinking, if deployed and supported appropriately, helps public-sector organizations not only improve internal efficiency but also significantly improve the effectiveness of programs and services in health, education, human services, public safety, the economy, the environment, and so on. For example, the State of Washington is using Lean to deliver its Results Washington goals of a world-class education, prosperous economy, sustainable energy and a clean environment, healthy and safe communities, and effective, efficient, and accountable government. Saskatchewan is using it to help achieve the "Saskatchewan Plan for Growth," a strategy designed to secure a better quality of life for all Saskatchewan people.

Those jurisdictions that use Lean extensively have a robust management and leadership environment, including political leadership, to support the initiative. They have a strong customer service orientation and use Lean as part of digital and direct service delivery to improve value for the customer. Strong public-sector Lean organizations have dedicated resources, centrally, to oversee improvement and, locally, to undertake improvement activity. In addition, they are committed to transparency and public reporting. Some also have private sector representation, partnerships or involvement tasked with providing advice on ways to offer better services more efficiently.

Clearly, governments are recognizing that it is imperative to improve the performance of public services to achieve better outcomes. They know that use of Lean is in the public interest.

What Is Lean?

Lean is a business philosophy with a set of tools, methods, and approaches that engage frontline employees, who do the work, to identify waste; improve processes, programs, and services; and problem-solve with their managers. Lean focuses on transactional business processes that deliver improvement at the operational level; and transformational change – in strategy, management, processes, culture, and systems – to achieve and sustain maximum performance. The term "Lean" refers to an absence of waste.

Elements of Lean thinking, as a system of production and management, go back as far as the Industrial Revolution. The Toyota Production System is credited with perfecting Lean. While it originated in the private sector in manufacturing, use of Lean has spread to logistics and distribution, financial services, retail, construction, maintenance, and healthcare. Now, Lean tools and principles are being adapted for the public sector with governments using Lean to renew public services.

Lean methodology is focused on delivering to customers exactly what they need, when they need it, in the quantity they need, in the right sequence, without defects, at the lowest possible cost. It aligns business processes with customer requirements, eliminates wasted time and effort from processes, and builds new processes, products, or services that meet customer and business requirements. It also puts in place the infrastructure, management, and leadership systems to sustain gains and foster continuous improvement.

Why Lean?

Lean enhances organizational performance. It gets to the root of problems and creates transparency for everyone – staff, management, and customers – so programs, services and processes can be improved for the customer's benefit. Key to Lean is employee engagement, customer service, and a focus on continuous improvement. Lean's focus on value, quality, and people leads to long-term behavioral change and cultural transformation. People within public-sector organizations are united in pursuit of a common direction and are driven by a desire to improve the customer experience. When applied to the public sector, Lean ultimately benefits everyone by creating better value for the investment of public dollars.

What Lean Isn't

Lean can help organizations improve their programs and services; however, it is not a mechanism for determining whether those programs and services are, in fact, appropriate. There is no point in "leaning" out a program

> *Lean is a way for us to ensure that we reduce waste, make the best use of our time, ensure that work is rewarding for our employees and not frustrating, and that they're not burdened with wasteful work and work that could be done much more efficiently*
> — Deputy Minister of Agriculture

that is no longer relevant or required. Program review and evaluation is the appropriate methodology for determining program or service need, not Lean.

Furthermore, Lean is not intended to interfere in professional relationships such as those among physician, nurse, and patient; between teacher and student; or between social worker and client. These are value-added interactions and the objective is to use Lean to enhance or "free-up" time for these important professional interventions.

> *Our government wants to engage employees and we want to hear their great ideas. Lean is a process that opens the dialogue. It lets all employees come forward with ideas to join in problem-solving teams so our services to the public are the very best they can be.*
> *- Minister Responsible for the Public Service Commission*

A common misconception about Lean is that it is simply a process improvement methodology. In fact, Lean is much more and should be used to change employees' mind-set about work: about what employees and managers do, how they do it, what tools they use to improve how work gets done, and how value is delivered to the customer.

Lean should not be viewed as a tool intended to fix problems when they arise. This perspective results in a focus on the methods and tools rather than a culture of continuous improvement. Lean is not a project. It is an ongoing journey with no specific end. When viewed as a project, Lean becomes burdensome to staff and managers. On the other hand, when it is viewed as "the way we work," Lean has a far-reaching impact on the organization.

Lean Principles and Waste

To understand Lean and how it can be used within an organization to enhance leadership, manage effectively, and foster a culture of continuous improvement, you must first learn about Lean principles, waste, and essential Lean methods.

There are five key principles essential for Lean thinking (Lean Enterprise Institute, 2009):

1. Focus on value from the standpoint of the end customer;
2. Identify all steps in the process or value stream, from start to finish, eliminating those that do not create value and are wasteful;
3. Make the steps in the process value-creating, occurring in tight sequence so the product or service flows smoothly toward the customer;

4. As flow is introduced, let customers pull value from the next upstream activity; and
5. Begin the process again to continuously improve by creating more value and further reducing waste.

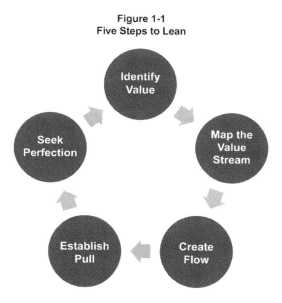

Figure 1-1
Five Steps to Lean

Key to Lean is exposing and eliminating waste. Waste exists everywhere in organizations, whether they are in the private, nonprofit, or public sector. Lean trains employees to identify and eliminate wasted time, energy, and activity in the workplace.

There are eight forms of waste in organizations. Examples include:

1. **Rework/Defects** – Correcting mistakes, doing the same inspection twice, producing multiple versions of what is basically the same document, and mislabeling specimens
2. **Overproduction** – Producing reports that are not required, photocopying material that is not needed, meeting for the sake of meeting, writing and reading long reports
3. **Overprocessing** – Capturing the same information many times, multiple levels of approval for a simple business expense, too much paperwork, too many meetings, unnecessary emails, time spent by professionals "perfecting" presentations

4. **Transportation** – Physically moving documents, information, or inventory unnecessarily
5. **Queues/Inventory** – Waiting lists, excessive stocking of forms and supplies, and backlogs of applications, claims, permits, invoices, or documents
6. **Movement/Motion** – Searching for documents, looking for supplies, unnecessary steps to access photocopier, looking for medication or equipment
7. **Waiting Time** – Idle time when people, equipment, or materials are not available when needed; for example, meetings start late, people are waiting to see the doctor, social worker, or principal, employees waiting for supervisory approval before proceeding to the next step
8. **Underutilized people** – Skills are not aligned with the tasks people perform, that is, professionals and senior managers performing administrative tasks, economists doing data entry (not realizing that is actually what they are doing), geologists undertaking basic financial analysis, nurses spending excessive time documenting

Lean Methods

There are a variety of Lean methods which can be deployed, depending on organizational needs. Some are simple, structured approaches; some are event-based; and others are advanced Lean methods. All address a particular problem identified by the organization.

Value Stream Mapping (VSM) Events

Value Stream Mapping (VSM) events are structured, intense, focused, process improvement projects that engage teams of employees, managers, customers, and clients over a period of four to five days to map out a process in detail from beginning to end (the current state); and identify issues and solutions for improvement (the future state). Key is the engagement of frontline staff who understand the details of a process, and customers or clients who are the recipients.

VSMs emphasize value and non-value-added process steps, delays, and handoffs. They are not just process maps; rather, they are a Lean technique to show all activities, information, and materials involved in a process, from start to finish, including suppliers and end customers. The start-to-finish process is the value stream – the steps that occur within an organization to deliver the product, service, or experience the customer wants or needs.

The product of a VSM is an implementation plan for continuous improvement which is implemented over a period of thirty, sixty, or ninety days.

CASE STUDY
Oil and Gas Technical Application

The Challenge
A Canadian province had a backlog of five hundred applications for horizontal well drilling. Private contractors had to wait up to six weeks for approval with equipment sitting idle at considerable expense.

The Strategy
A Lean Value Stream Mapping event was undertaken to map out existing processes and develop a future state for improvement. This included creation of a single levy, which replaced ten licenses and permits.

The Results
Industry wait times were reduced from up to six weeks to less than two weeks, and the backlog of applications was eliminated. Oil companies can now apply for a permit and, in one day, receive a license to drill. The time to conduct a technical review was also reduced from more than thirty days to one. Twenty thousand transactions have been eliminated and incomplete applications have been reduced from 50 percent to 5 percent. Most importantly, a record number of horizontal wells were drilled in 2013, which provided significant benefit to the local economy.

The Future
Sustaining the improved climate for doing business is key to the province's continuing prosperity. It will be important to sustain the gains made in the oil and gas sector.

Rapid Process Improvement Workshops (RPI)/Kaizen Events

Because of its origins with Toyota, Lean sometimes uses Japanese terms to describe concepts. *Kaizen* events, also known as RPIs (Rapid Process Improvement), are focused improvement efforts which deliver immediate benefit because changes are implemented during the event itself. They are undertaken between one and five days and identify areas for rapid improvement and reduction of waste. *Kaizen* events sometimes jumpstart larger, sustained improvement efforts (United States Environmental Protection Agency, 2013).

CASE STUDY
A Canadian Medical Laboratory

The Challenge
Outpatients visiting a medical lab between 8 a.m. to 10 a.m. were waiting too long to have their blood drawn. The average wait time was thirty-six minutes. Administrators wanted to reduce this wait time by 50 percent.

The Strategy
A Rapid Process Improvement event was undertaken. Healthcare providers and patients were engaged to develop and implement changes, which would reduce waiting time. Changes introduced included altering the hours of staff, adjusting the lab requisition intake process, and improving signage.

The Results
Waiting time was reduced from thirty-six to seventeen minutes. Patients no longer have to wait extended periods before blood is drawn and can continue with their schedule for the day.

The Future
The laboratory will continue to monitor waiting time to ensure the improvements are sustained.

Mistake Proofing

Mistake proofing uses Lean methodology to examine the root causes of errors and aims to prevent them before they create defects (for example, an error that is passed down the line to a patient). It can also eliminate rework and reduce costs. In the public sector, mistakes can result from a variety of factors such as poor communication, lack of training, human fatigue, defective equipment, and a lack of standards, rules, policies, and procedures.

> ## CASE STUDY
> ## Mistake Proofing in a Hospital
>
> ### The Challenge
> Medication errors were occurring on all units within a hospital because of the lack of staff signature. Contributing factors included nurses being interrupted by patients and colleagues; a lack of standard procedures for administering medication; paper-based, manual documentation; and information regarding medication errors not being shared. Patients expect their medications to be administered correctly.
>
> ### The Strategy
> A mistake proofing event was undertaken to eliminate medication errors related to a missing staff signature. This included the creation of standard work on how to administer medications, a Lean improvement event for the medications room and storage, creation of a standardized medication cart, use of visuals to minimize interruptions, and changes to the medication administration record.
>
> ### The Results
> There was an 80 percent reduction in "no signature" errors. Also, there was increased staff engagement as the project progressed and greater awareness about the inherent risk of medication errors.
>
> ### The Future
> New practices will be sustained through daily management and an audit process has been put in place to monitor and ensure the improvements are sustained.

Six Sigma

Lean Six Sigma is a process improvement approach used when problems can be identified through numerical data. It is oriented to removing the cause of efforts or defects and variability in processes. It uses quality management methods that are often statistically based and follow DMAIC, an acronym for Define, Measure Analyze, Improve, and Control. The DMAIC improvement cycle is the core tool used to drive Six Sigma projects methodology of defining the problem, measuring and analyzing process data, improving the process, and controlling the future state to correct deviations (United States Environmental Protection Agency, 2013).

CASE STUDY
Claims Front End Process Improvement
Workplace Injury Claims Processing

The Challenge
The claims front end process area in a workplace injury insurance organization receives more than ten thousand paper documents from injured workers and employers on a daily basis. The documents must be sorted, scanned, and indexed to the correct claim file to ensure that the appropriate case manager receives and processes the documents in a timely manner. The document scan and index process was not meeting customer expectations for timeliness and accuracy. End-users of the claims system were complaining that they spent far too long looking for documents, which reduced the time they spent handling their caseloads and dealing with their client needs. The problems with the process included:
- High error rates in indexing accuracy, quality, and registration of certain documents on the mainframe; and
- Delays in document indexing cycle time.

The Approach
Lean Six Sigma Define, Measure, Analyze, Improve and Control (DMAIC) methodology, tools, and techniques were applied in this project. The consultants provided team leadership support throughout the five phases of the DMAIC methodology as well as Just in Time training and coaching.

There was an overall document indexing, quality, and mainframe document registration error rate of 38.5 percent in the process. The sigma level of this process (a measure of process capability _ the higher the sigma-level, the more capable the process is) was 1.82σ. The mean cycle time for document indexing was 62.3 hours and the upper specification limit was twenty-four hours. This resulted in a sigma level for cycle time of -1.23σ. Improving these processes would also reduce delays associated with handling caseloads, increase the efficiency of the end-users, increase their productivity, drive down unit costs, and reduce the cycle time associated with processing claims.

The Results
Upon completion of the project, the business realized the following tangible and intangible benefits:

1. Reduced the overall document cycle time from sixty-two hours to less than twenty-four hours;
2. Reduced document registration error rate from 38.5 percent to less than 5 percent;
3. Increased sigma level of the process to 2.8σ; and
4. Improved staff confidence and satisfaction.

5S

5S is a method for maintaining a clean and organized workplace. It is based on steps to:

1. Sort: organize materials and retain only what's essential;
2. Set in Order ("a place for everything and everything in its place");
3. Shine (clean and straighten);
4. Standardize (spread improvements to all worksites or workstations); and
5. Sustain (ensure maintenance and review of standards).

Some organizations add a sixth "S" for Safety.

5S is a systematic way to involve frontline employees to gain control of information, equipment, material, and inventory in furtherance of an organized, clean, healthy, safe, and high-performing workplace (Pricewaterhouse Coopers (PwC), 2014).

CASE STUDY
5S in a Canadian Highways Ministry

The Challenge

Keeping a highway department's repair depots and maintenance shops safe and in good condition is important since the less time equipment is in the shop, the more time it can be used to maintain roads. Yet shops were cluttered and filled with equipment that was old, in disrepair, and no longer being utilized. Also, yards had not been cleaned up in years.

The Strategy

To keep its shops organized and running efficiently the Ministry held a series of 5S events in its repair depots and maintenance shops.

Part of the process included examining the steps taken in the maintenance process. There was a very inefficient layout and large distances traveled between steps.

In one maintenance shop alone, twenty-six disposal bins were filled with about 27,300 cubic feet of waste. This was equivalent to filling almost eight large semi-trailer trucks.

Ministry of Highways Employee Testimonials

I'm old school. I'm used to tools in toolboxes. I was skeptical at first and heard rumors that they threw everything out. But it was nothing bad like that at all. We replaced worn-out tools, got rid of clutter, and made it easier to get around in the shops.

We used to run around like chickens with our heads cut off. Our tools resembled the kitchen drawer – you know, the one where ice picks and egg flippers and tongs are all jammed together and you can't find a thing. Well now, our diagnostic carts are outlined on the floor and every pin, screw, and gadget has a place. All the stuff you need to do the job is right where you need it. You don't have to keep walking back and forth trying to find things.

If we get a call at 10 p.m. that there's been an accident, the last thing we want to do is scramble to find the right signs if we have to close a road. It just makes sense to know where the right signs, barricades, and pylons are and have them easily accessible.

> **The Results**
> The ministry has seen marked improvements:
>
> - The repair depots have cut more than 1 million dollars in costs and have reduced truck downtime from nine to four days.
> - Another 350,000 dollars in cost avoidance has resulted from 5S in maintenance shops. In addition, more efficient access to tools and materials has reduced the steps to complete an oil change and greasing by up to 88 percent.
>
> The ministry has substantially improved the safety of the workplace and, by protecting supplies and scheduling preventive maintenance, it has extended the life of its equipment.
>
> **The Future**
> The ministry intends to have two-thirds of all shops complete 5S in the next three to five years (it has eighty-four maintenance locations). To sustain gains made as a result of using 5S, the ministry has put in place an annual audit process. Managers are now conducting audits, identifying shortfalls, and creating plans to correct deficiencies.

3P

3P is an advanced Lean method for designing or redesigning new space or products. The Production, Preparation Process (3P) seeks to meet customer needs by starting with a clean slate and designing a new process as simple and waste-free as possible, while anticipating and addressing potential problems. It goes beyond the continued improvement of existing processes to make "quantum leap" design improvements to improve performance.

CASE STUDY
New Canadian Regional Hospital

The Challenge
A Canadian Health Region was replacing its hospital. It wanted a modern, state-of-the-art healthcare facility that put the needs of patients and families first. It embarked on a 3P process to streamline the seven flows of medicine: of patients, providers, supplies, medications, equipment, information, and process engineering. Goals were to eliminate waste, maximize flexibility and adaptability, break down department silos, reduce complexity, make the new facility easier to use and maintain, and eliminate process steps.

The Strategy
The Health Region brought together its architect with doctors, administrators, nurses, facility managers, maintenance workers, patients, and families. Together they designed the new hospital space with a focus on quality care, patient and employee safety, and the "flow" of patients and supplies. Tabletop model mock-ups were built to test and refine the space design. The Health Region leased a warehouse and then built actual-size mock-ups of the proposed new space, including furniture and equipment. Leadership used 3P because they were reimagining from the ground up, compared to working toward a predetermined design and outcome.

The Results
Construction of the new hospital is complete and it has opened. The entire healthcare team is unified and excited that their new facility was built according to their own design.

> I am now a believer in these processes our hospitals are using to make things better for patients and families. I trust that they have me in mind, as a regular user of the health care system....It will renew your faith in our health-care system. It certainly did for me.
> _ Patient participant in a 3P event

The Future
Operational cost savings of between eighty-five million dollars to 160 million dollars are anticipated over the next twenty years.

A3

Project plans or strategies, called A3s due to the size of 11-inch x 17-inch paper (A3) they are displayed upon, tell the story of how an improvement effort will address critical needs and gaps. They articulate root causes; define activities, timelines, and resources; and set out measures and targets. The structured approach assists in problem solving, action planning, monitoring and adjusting deployment, and the measurement of results.

Visual Controls

Visual controls are signs, controls, or symbols in the workplace that remind people of standard procedures, reinforce safety, provide feedback on performance, and hold people accountable. Visual workplaces are clean, well-organized, and efficient. Recognizing that "a picture tells a thousand words," Lean workplaces use photographs and signage to convey "at a glance" information such as how to operate devices, show where things are stored, manage cues, control inventory, illustrate the status of work, identify hazards, make abnormalities obvious, and mistake-proof the organization.

Strategy Deployment/Hoshin Kanri

Hoshin Kanri is a methodology for linking strategic planning with strategy deployment. It identifies outcomes, goals, and priorities; designates people, resources, and timeframes for project completion; establishes project metrics; and cascades deployment throughout an organization or sector to ensure everyone involved "thinks and acts as one."

CASE STUDY
Using *Hoshin Kanri* Across Saskatchewan's Education Sector

The Challenge

In 2013-14, the incoming Deputy Minister of Education, also the Deputy Minister Responsible for Lean, recognized it was imperative to deal head-on with significant issues in education in the province of Saskatchewan. Only 74 percent of students were graduating on time and, even worse, only 36 percent of First Nations and Métis students were graduating. Credit attainment was poor and the province was not doing well when compared nationally or internationally.

The ministry, school divisions, and educational stakeholders were working independently to achieve improvements in K-12 education across the province. There was no unifying vision or plan; instead, each organization had its own plan, which was not necessarily aligned with the priorities of the Government of Saskatchewan. Furthermore, at a time when resources were very tight, there was little sharing across the system, and few standardized processes were in place.

The deputy minister launched "Student First" to improve teaching and learning, and enhance the effectiveness and efficiency of the entire education sector.

The Strategy

Hoshin Kanri was used to bring together more than one thousand people to develop the first ever collaboratively developed province-wide plan for deployment across the education sector. All public and Catholic school divisions; the Conseil des Écoles Fransaskoises; First Nations and Métis partners; ministry staff, school boards, and students were involved.

The following strategic intent, or "true north," originally developed by a group of grade six students, was adopted for 2014 to 2020:

- *I am ready to learn:* I am safe, healthy, and hopeful.
- *I am valued:* I have a voice and am supported in my ways of learning.
- *I belong:* I contribute, am respected, and respectful.
- *I am successful:* at levels appropriate for my ability and aspiration.
- *I am preparing for my future:* in education, in employment, in my community, and in life.

Six enduring strategies were then identified as foundational. These were the broad areas of strategic focus that defined "What's in" and "What's out" of the *Hoshin Kanri* plan. Enduring strategies were thought of as the "Big How."

Five outcomes were then identified as the "destination" or "big dot" targets the sector was trying to achieve over the next five years or more. They reflected the results those involved wanted to see. Outcomes were stated in terms of *what* the desired improvement/change was, *when* it was to be achieved, and *how much* was to be improved.

Once the outcomes were identified, the next step was to identify improvement targets to act as a link between the outcomes and the breakthrough *hoshins*. While the targets in the outcomes section were long-term outcome measures, those in the improvement target section needed to be medium-term process measures that relied on data that was more frequently and readily available. The group considered: *What are the improvement targets that will enable us to achieve our outcomes? What are the specific things we need to do to get to the outcomes? What are the performance measures that we have to improve?*

The group then identified two "must do, can't fail" breakthrough *hoshins* for the year. These were seen as vital short-term projects which required discipline to complete _ to "focus and finish."

The Results

Upon completion of the plan, all twenty-eight school boards approved it, as did the Government of Saskatchewan. All also agreed to cascade the plan within their organization so deployment could begin in 2014_2015. Resources are now in place to sustain the initiative, and Lean events are underway within individual organizations, and across the sector, to support improvement. Significant results are already being realized. In the first two years of the initiative, grade 3 students reading at or above grade level rose from 65 percent to 74 percent (CBC Saskatchewan, 2016). These results are not a sample, but rather a census of every grade 3 student in the province.

The Future

Further engagement will occur to strengthen and deploy the plan, through ongoing conversations with students, parents, teachers, and Student First advisors who have been appointed by the Government. The goal is to engage twenty-three thousand educators and support staff, administrators, First Nations and Métis organizations, community organizations, and parents and students.

Moving forward, each school division, the ministry, and other identified partners will develop and deploy their own plans, which will feed into continued improvement of the education sector plan.

Lean Management

Lean Management is a structured approach to uniting an organization's staff and processes in support of its objectives or *hoshin* plan. Lean Management equips frontline supervisors, managers, and leaders with the skills and tools they need to lead and manage effectively, and to foster a culture of continuous improvement. Leaders engage with their staff to empower their employees to solve problems they encounter in their everyday work. They exercise discipline to ensure rigor in the identification of problems and root cause analysis, the deployment of plans, and the measurement of results. Leadership behaviors are adjusted to focus on mentoring, coaching, and training. (See Chapter 5 for a full discussion of leading, managing, and strategic use of Lean.)

Chapter 2

THE CUSTOMER AND CITIZEN

Who Is the Customer?

One of the reasons we are strong supporters of Lean is the emphasis it places on the customer and on improving the customer experience throughout a value stream. All activities in a value stream are viewed through the eye of the customer and improvements are designed accordingly. This is ideal for public services, which, by their very nature, are about serving a "public" customer.

However, many government employees do not even realize they have a customer. While the notions of customer and customer service are pervasive in the private sector, we have experienced blank stares when we've asked public workers to identify their customers.

In our experience, public employees are strongly motivated by a desire to provide quality, professional public services. This is at the very heart of what they do and why many have chosen to work in the public rather than the private sector. Public servants are intrinsically motivated to deliver excellent service and Lean is ideal to meet that goal. It actively engages them in finding ways to serve their customer better. In so doing, it also makes their work more rewarding.

> Staff find it personally rewarding to place our clients first. Our work as a team helped us to address the issues that we faced.
> _ Ministry of Social Services employee

But identifying the "customer" of public services can be challenging. For example, is the client of a human resources department the manager who receives HR support, or the employee who works for the organization? Furthermore, depending on the particular service being provided, language is important. In the public sector, customers can be citizens, clients, students, patients, employers, industry, and so on. For the purposes of this book, we've interwoven use of these terms but we recognize that employees, managers, and executives have clear preferences about what term is used and in what circumstances. A corporation that applies for a permit to drill a horizontal well, for example, would be considered a "customer." A low-income citizen applying for financial assistance becomes a "client" once he or she is deemed eligible.

In the public sector there are usually many different interests at stake – people who access programs and services as well as a variety of stakeholders, including employees, advocacy groups, regulatory bodies, elected officials, and, of course, the taxpayer. Generally speaking, it is possible to differentiate between those who receive services – customers – and those who influence the delivery of those services – whom we call stakeholders.

But the customer of a process may also be internal to the public service. For example, the customer of the budget development process in the UK government is, ultimately, the Treasury Board and Cabinet; similarly, the customer of a procurement process may be a government employee who requires a new computer. From a Lean perspective, recognizing both internal and external customers is important.

When improving programs and services in the public sector, it is necessary to consider the interests of internal and external customers, as well as those of stakeholders. However, we would argue that those of the external customer are paramount since they are truly the recipient of the public service.

Lean adds value through improved and safer service for citizens. It adds value for employees who are better able to deliver needed services thereby providing them with the satisfaction of seeing improved outcomes for the people they serve. In addition, governments see value through more efficient use of people and financial resources. Lean is a "win-win" for all involved.

Voice of the Customer

We can't emphasize enough the importance of hearing and understanding the voice of the customer. In the public sector, the perspective of the customer is often taken for granted. Employees, advocacy groups, and other stakeholders represent what they believe to be in the client's best interests when, sometimes, they are in fact misinformed or have interests of their own which interfere with their ability to be objective. This is particularly true of programs and services aimed at the most vulnerable members of society, such as people with disabilities and the poor, who may not have the personal and organizational resources to represent themselves.

> *This experience was very empowering. I am confident patients are being listened to. This is a game-changer for the patients*
> — Patient participant in a Saskatchewan Rapid Process Improvement Event

Identifying the customer and defining value from the standpoint of that customer is the first step in Lean transformation (Womack and Jones, 1996). Citizens and users of public services want a say in how to make things better. Public expectations of government are increasing, in part, as a result of experience with a more responsive, technologically advanced private sector. People are accustomed to placing an order online and "chatting" with customer service representatives and they increasingly expect to do the same when accessing government programs. Hearing directly from the customer can be accomplished in a variety of ways such as through traditional complaints mechanisms, whether they be by telephone, online, or in person, or through proactive approaches which reach out to the customer such as through interviews, focus groups, surveys, direct observation, and participation in Lean improvement events. Understanding the customer experience, including their digital experience, is a critical part of achieving results that matter.

In the Saskatchewan healthcare system, for example, there is a target to have patient and family representatives participate in 100 percent of Lean process improvements focused on making the patient experience better (that is, Rapid Process Improvement, Value Stream Mapping, 5S, or 3P events). Clearly, Saskatchewan healthcare leaders recognize the value of hearing the voice of the customer. This is because of an inherent tendency to design service in response to the needs of providers, particularly physicians, rather than those of patients.

There are four attributes that are particularly important to customers: quality of the product or service, speed of delivery, safety, and corporate responsibility (which includes ethical conduct, privacy, legal compliance, and so on). In both the public and private sector, these quality parameters are balanced against a need to deliver at low cost with few resources.

The Customer at the Center?

In the private sector, knowing who the customers are and understanding what they want and need lead to delivery of a product or service that responds accordingly. In the public sector, designing an appropriate response is more confusing.

As governments around the world discuss renewing and refreshing public services, they use language such as "citizen-centered service delivery," "citizen first," and "putting the customer at the center." This is in recognition that, over time, public services have sometimes lost sight of the customer and have not kept up with public expectations, particularly when it comes to speed of delivery and use of technology.

But putting the customer at the center of service delivery loses sight of the fact that the relationship between the provider of the service and the customer may not be equal in the public sector. Furthermore, there can be an inherent conflict between the interests of the customer and those of the broader public.

Take social assistance, for example. The client comes seeking financial support, while the public good is financial independence. The compromise may be making financial support conditional upon job search. Furthermore, an additional public service, that of employment assistance, is provided to support employment efforts. In reality, the nature of the services provided reflect the fact that the two parties – government and client – have entered into a partnership or social contract.

Bert Teeuwen, in his book *Lean for the Public Sector: The Pursuit of Perfection in Government Services*, distinguishes among seven citizen roles: customers, users, subjects, voters, taxpayers, partners, and administrators (Teeuwen, 2010):

Figure 2-1

Citizen and Government Roles[1]			
	Citizen Role	**Role of Government**	**Example**
Customers	Citizens who choose a service	To provide the service	Mail Public transport
Users	Of public facilities	To regulate and maintain public facilities	Parks
Subjects	Subject to laws and enforcement	To legislate and enforce in the public interest	Building permits Traffic laws Environmental protection
Voters	Represented by political decision-making	To ensure fair, orderly elections and represent voters	Federal, provincial and municipal elections Referenda
Taxpayers	Pay tax to support public services	To levy tax	Provincial tax Fuel tax
Partners	Collaborate with government in development/delivery	To engage citizens in development/delivery	Citizen involvement in city planning Public-private-partnerships
Administrators	Citizens who become politically active to influence	To facilitate citizen representation on committees/boards	City Council Boards of Education University Senate

Citizens are always parties to the provision of a government program or service by being customers, users, and subjects, as well as taxpayers. However, citizens, as members of the public, also have a concomitant interest in the public good. Consequently, when undertaking a service improvement, a balance needs to be found between citizen as customer and the public interest.

Engaging the Citizen

A foundational principle of Lean is focusing on value from the standpoint of the end customer. This requires a deep understanding of the customer experience. Just as strong organizations respect and engage their employees, so too should they respect and engage their customer. The needs and concerns of clients should inform improvement efforts.

---

[1] Adapted from Teeuwen (2010)

The Institute for Citizen-Centred Service in Canada, a not-for-profit organization that works with governments to pursue partnerships and coordinate initiatives focused on innovative public-sector service delivery, advocates for governments to move away from an inside-out approach, where services are designed in accordance with what an organization sees as important, to an outside-in approach, where services are based on citizens' needs and expectations. They advocate direct involvement of citizens, where possible, to ensure improvement is sensitive and responsive to client needs.

The International Association of Public Participation, an international association to promote and improve the practice of public participation in relation to individuals, governments, and institutions that affect the public interest, describes five levels of citizen engagement and the corresponding "promise" to the public for that engagement depending upon its goal or purpose.

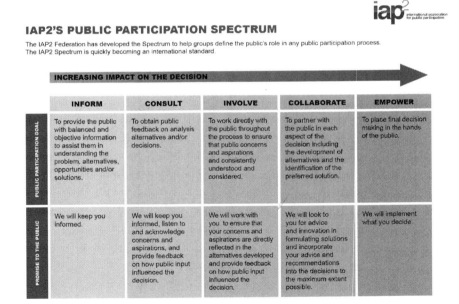

This spectrum (International Association of Public Participation Spectrum 2017) is becoming an international standard for public participation. On the left, public service organizations inform and provide information, or consult and ask for input. Increased engagement incorporates public perspectives in the development of alternatives, and collaboration includes working directly with clients and customers to frame issues and solve problems. In Washington State, for example, the governor has met directly with the homeless to seek their perspective; and, in Saskatchewan, patients, students, and offenders have been directly involved in Lean improvement events. Organizations can use Lean to increase citizen engagement to incorporate, collaborate, and empower. Lean methods can be used to actively engage clients in improvement, including codesign of programs and services.

CASE STUDY
Washington State Correctional Industries

Washington State Correctional Industries (CI) is a state-operated business located within Washington State Department of Corrections. Its mandate is to maintain and expand work training programs for offenders, develop marketable job skills, instill and promote positive work ethics, and reduce the tax burden of corrections. CI operates over forty service, manufacturing, and agricultural industries within eleven correctional facilities throughout the state (Washington State Correctional Industries, 2014).

In 2007, CI began implementing Lean manufacturing principles with the goals of reducing waste and establishing best practices. Staff at every facility learned to identify opportunities to reduce delays, minimize waste and scrap, cut costs, and increase value to the customer (Washington State Correctional Industries, 2013). CI is now in the process of expanding Lean implementation to engage its inmate population directly in Lean improvement.

The Challenge

As part of its ongoing commitment to post-release employment, Correctional Industries has initiated a pilot project to create a Lean job description and classification for incarcerated workers employed in about sixty shops within Correctional Industries. The purpose is to create a job classification that is considered highly desirable by the private business sector so the training and Lean experience obtained by inmates while incarcerated will enable them to gain meaningful employment upon their release. While they are applying their Lean skills and expertise in the CI shops, they will also be improving the internal operational efficiency of the facility. If successful, the project should also enhance the working relationships between CI workers and state employees with whom they interact.

The Approach

CI anticipates recruiting more than twenty-five Continuous Improvement Clerks from within the inmate population across the state. The new Continuous Improvement Clerks, once trained, will:

- Provide Lean training to their co-workers with CI;
- Implement and monitor 5S (workplace cleanliness and organization) programs at all sites;
- Assist in the development of visual shop floor key performance indicators;
- Assist in the collection and analysis of existing performance data that will provide measures and help to establish performance goals;
- Facilitate *Kaizen* continuous improvement events to strengthen processes and enhance efficiency; and
- Develop monthly progress reports.

Prior to and following release the Clerks will receive assistance to secure and maintain employment.

To develop the new positions, collaboration was required between the CI management team (senior leadership team, general managers, business managers, and workforce development specialists) and the custody staff (corrections officers and sergeants). Meetings were held to discuss development of the job description, scope, pay scale, reporting structure, location of work station, movement schedules, dress/attire, and so on. Compromises were made and agreements reached.

To get started, CI has initiated a pilot project at Coyote Ridge Corrections Center. Two new Continuous Improvement Clerks have been recruited and selected from the inmate population; they report to shop floor supervisors and managers (who are state employees) responsible for normal operations. The new clerks are being mentored and coached by the state's Continuous Improvement manager responsible for Coyote Ridge.

CI began by training some Coyote Ridge shop supervisors on Lean. The new Continuous Improvement Clerks assisted in developing training materials and the process for recruiting and selecting offenders to participate in the twenty hours of Lean training. Shop supervisors were initially skeptical; however, as they began to see the benefit of having additional resources for improvement, they became more interested, supportive, and engaged. The idea of creating the Continuous Improvement Clerk position was an innovative approach to providing a unique skill set for the incarcerated individuals within CI. The positions empower workers to facilitate change within their respective shops, which is an unconventional approach given the environment of the corrections facility. The initiative has energized both those working as Continuous Improvement Clerks and the general worker population.

There were, and continue to be, challenges to initiating and sustaining the pilot project. A clear chain of command and reporting structure has been developed to manage initial confusion about the roles and responsibilities of the clerks and staff. Culture change among the state's custody staff to reinforce CI's trained inmates as future valued members of society is a work in progress since the staff, understandably, is mainly interested in accountability and compliance. Shop supervisors have varying levels of interest and understanding of Lean Manufacturing and, until they are all fully trained, their level of involvement will be mixed. For security reasons, the Continuous Improvement Clerks do not have access to the internet and, as a result, must create their own documentation and training aids, or seek support from the facility's Continuous Improvement Manager. Demand for such support could be challenging as the pilot project expands and more Continuous Improvement Clerks are recruited.

Going forward, CI recognizes that the selection of appropriate candidates for Continuous Improvement Clerks will be critical to success of the initiative _ both for securing and sustaining post-release employment, and for the continuous improvement of internal operations and work culture. They will need to consider factors such as time left on sentence, infraction history, time spent with CI, temperament, education level, and overall competence.

The Results

It is too early to determine all the benefits of the project. To date, the new Continuous Improvement Clerks have received forty hours of Lean Practitioner training and are presently working on improvement projects in an effort to earn their "Practitioner Certification" through CI's Continuous Improvement branch. The clerks have successfully delivered twenty hours of "Fundamentals of Lean Manufacturing" training for twenty-three workers and one staff at the pilot site. Nine operational improvement initiatives have also been undertaken and are being monitored to capture cost savings, cost avoidance, new capacity/productivity gains, revenue growth, service improvement, and quality improvement. Annual savings for 2016 are estimated at 112,000 dollars.

CI reports that, at Coyote Ridge, there has been an increase in suggestions coming forward from workers using the language commonly associated with Lean. Managers and supervisors are beginning to understand the importance of capturing baseline information to measure the current state and to frame improvement. Staff is also using more visual indicators to help manage their work and understand day-to-day performance issues. A stronger focus on performance measurement is reported along with conversations about the quality of Key Performance Indicators (KPIs) and of how performance is rated. Shops are 50 percent cleaner and daily audits are driving that percentage higher. Clutter and waste has been discovered and addressed, and material costs reduced. Supervisors are more visible on the floor, giving workers more opportunity to put forward their ideas for improvement.

As CI expands the pilot project, culture change is expected within CI statewide. A new way of thinking with respect to how workers conduct themselves while incarcerated is anticipated, and it is hoped that knowledge gained through the CI Lean environment will be transferable to the private sector and the community as a whole. CI's target is for 100 percent of all staff and incarcerated individuals to receive Lean training. Information centers, called huddle boards, have been developed to make visible how corporate strategic goals are aligned with onsite KPIs. They provide a combination of lagging and leading indicators to track safety, quality, delivery, and cost (SQDC) and to provide a platform to inform and broaden employee understanding of their role.

Ultimately, CI plans to continue on its Lean journey as part of its commitment to enhancing post-release employment, reducing recidivism, and achieving operational efficiencies. This will, in turn, benefit all citizens of Washington State.

Testimonial: Continuous Improvement Clerk

I would like to give you my impressions of the program to date and what it means to me personally.

When we talk about culture within these walls we must understand that it is deeply rooted at an institutional level. Inmates are dehumanized from the beginning of their incarceration, in many cases with good reason. What is left at the end of the typical incarceration period is an individual unsuited to life outside of prison.

People who are incarcerated adapt to their environment as any human would, becoming more violent, or more apathetic, or more sedate; whatever the situation these climates have, they are usually not conducive to providing stimulus that encourages pro-social behavior.

What Correctional industries (CI) is doing with Lean Manufacturing is changing that environment for the inmates. It encourages us to think, to challenge the way things have always been done. It demands that we become part of the culture CI wants to develop; one that values individuals and their observations no matter their status or level in life. This meets with much cultural bias from not only institutional staff but the inmate population as well.

For me, this program has been life-altering, giving me back a feeling of self-worth. I am constantly reminded that I am valued, that my opinion matters and that I am not a disposable person. It has revitalized a portion of my brain, allowing me to think again and to view the world from a positive perspective.

Chapter 3

THE LEAN JOURNEY

In the previous chapters, we have characterized implementation of Lean in the public sector as a journey without an end. It begins with an organizational assessment and continues to the point at which there is a fully embedded Lean culture and approach, with "endless" continuous improvement. Whether they are a department, ministry, a corporation owned by government, a health authority, a school division, or a post-secondary institution, public-sector organizations can anticipate going through five distinct phases as part of their Lean journey. They will assess, mobilize, initiate, integrate, and sustain.

Figure 3-1 The Five Phases of a Lean Journey

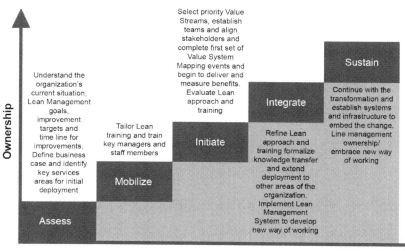

Phase 1: Strategy and Assessment

An organization's Lean journey usually begins following an organizational assessment that has concluded the organization needs to improve programs, services, and processes. The suggestion that Lean be selected as the methodology happens when senior change agents within the organization have already been exposed to Lean and therefore are likely to advocate its use.

Generally, a business case is prepared for moving forward. This includes identifying the rationale, resource requirements, and implementation approach which are proposed. Of course, the approach will depend upon the size and nature of the public service. The business case need not be a detailed cost-benefit analysis but simply, a list of key metrics that need to be improved. Metrics may include outcome and output measures of, for example, cost reduction, service improvement, new capacity creation, and so on. Key questions senior leadership need to answer are: What problems do we have? What improvements are we seeking? How much improvement are we seeking and by when? Answers to these questions will help establish the framework for the Lean journey, including how projects get selected and on which areas the organization needs to focus.

Once a decision has been made to proceed, a deployment strategy and the necessary resources need to be put in place to drive the initiative internally. Leadership and governance are key for communicating the vision, outlining expectations, securing resources, managing change, monitoring rollout, and measuring outcomes. In Washington State, for example, Lean is driven from the Governor's office.

Senior management leadership and support is critical and, very early in phase 1, it is necessary to secure a commitment from leaders to participate. This is sometimes a challenge since, without training, senior managers will not necessarily understand to what they are committing themselves! In some jurisdictions this has been managed, in part, by mandating the participation of ministries, departments, or service providers. Other organizations have used incentives such as leadership recognition to "pull" participation. However, we've seen numerous failures when use of Lean has been made optional for senior management and consequently, it has not been uniformly adopted across the entire organization. Senior management needs to be united in its pursuit of improvement or the Lean initiative is unlikely to be successful.

> The Chief Executive Officer of a prominent crown corporation reluctantly agreed to implement Lean in his organization. He made adoption by senior managers optional in their respective divisions. The vice president of the largest division, which accounted for more than 70 percent of the organization's activity, opted out. The organization went ahead and spent millions of dollars in training and improvement projects. Needless to say, the improvements were mediocre and Lean implementation was eventually terminated. It is important for senior management to understand what Lean is all about and what it can potentially do for the organization.

Regardless of whether participation is mandated or voluntary, executive-level training early in the process will help leaders understand Lean and its potential. It will also lead to a common understanding and language for improvement, and help the executive team to begin to identify priority areas for Lean improvement.

In addition, in our experience, dedicating internal resources with authority to work across the organization is also required. Most of the time, these internal resources are supplemented with external Lean consulting expertise at the beginning of the initiative. Different jurisdictions have taken varying approaches to procuring consulting expertise with some selecting a single provider and others choosing several. We recommend the former approach since governments generally find it easier to manage a single contract with clear accountability, and they can implement a consistent language and approach across multiple departments and sectors. This process is much more challenging when there are multiple firms, contracts, and accountability arrangements, and when firms use different language and approaches.

Over time, it is possible for public-sector organizations to grow internal capacity and wean themselves from being reliant on consultants. Typically they become self-sufficient over a period of two to three years, depending on the number of internal resources assigned, and the staff's ability to quickly learn and internalize the skills required to become internal Lean leaders.

Phase 2: Mobilization

Launch begins with the announcement that the organization is committed to improvement and transformation, and Lean is being implemented as the approach to achieving this improvement. Lean has been chosen in order to develop better service, improved safety, and increased efficiency. At this stage, it is also important to reinforce to employees that Lean can make their work more rewarding by better utilizing their talents, and by making it easier for them to serve customers more effectively.

> When I first heard I was going to be involved in a Lean project, I was hesitant because I thought Lean meant finding ways to cut jobs. Once I learned more about Lean, I saw firsthand that it is not at all about cutting jobs, but about finding ways to work more effectively to serve our clients.
> _Ministry of Labour Relations and Workplace Safety Employee

It's also important to explain what Lean isn't; it is not a mechanism for workforce reduction or public-sector downsizing. Employee participation and engagement is essential to the success of Lean and if the employees believe it could lead to a loss of jobs, they will do everything possible to undermine the initiative and they will refuse to participate. Communications need to be direct and clear on this point and if an organization is going through a downsizing exercise, it may be preferable to delay Lean implementation until the workforce reduction is accomplished or, at the very least, be clear that other means will be found to achieve reduction, not Lean.

> ...we work smarter, not harder, and the more we work with Lean, the more improvement we see.
> _Ministry of Health Employee

There should also be a conversation about Lean with union representatives, if applicable. In at least two public-sector organizations using Lean, unions were invited to participate directly in Lean training. This was immediately followed by a Lean event aimed at improving the grievance process. Since then, neither organization has been challenged by a union about its use of Lean.

Earlier, we mentioned the importance of executive-level Lean training. Every senior executive should be trained within the first month of mobilization and no executive should be permitted to opt out. As leaders, their job will be to drive implementation within their department or branch. They need to understand Lean so they are able to communicate its potential, champion implementation, and select programs, services, and processes which will benefit from Lean methods. A Lean mantra is "see – learn– do" and, as quickly as possible, senior leaders should see it in operation, learn about its potential and take on a Lean project to gain further understanding and appreciation on how the organization will benefit from using Lean.

Mobilizing Lean requires engagement of the entire workforce and, therefore, training is required for managers, supervisors, and frontline employees. Depending on the size of the workforce, this may take some time but there are a variety of ways to reach employees including formal training sessions, new employee orientations, online training, train-the-trainer approaches, and everyday inclusion of Lean content in communications and interactions. The approach selected will depend upon the organization's internal capacity and readiness for change.

A final point about mobilization – leaders (from frontline supervisors and managers to senior executives) need to be seen and heard. They need to be walking the *Gemba*, a Japanese term which refers to seeing the work directly by going to the floor, the frontline or the work area. They need to champion Lean in the workplace, engage directly with employees about Lean, solicit ideas for improvement, coach and mentor staff, problem solve operational issues daily, ensure standard work is practiced, measure performance, conduct daily staff discussions or huddles, and make sure success is recognized and celebrated.

Phase 3: Initiation

Phase 3 begins with the identification and selection of the initial value streams which will be subject to Lean improvement events. In our experience, organizations can get bogged down at this stage trying to determine with which value streams to start. We believe the most important thing is to keep it simple and *just get started*. At this stage, the organization needs to get some hands-on experience with Lean in order to see how Lean methods are applied and what can be accomplished. Improvement will be seen, early on, and as the organization gets more experience it can select more complex, strategic value streams. (See Chapter 5 for further information on strategic value stream selection.)

Once the initial value streams are identified, project charters are developed specifying the nature of the problem; goals, outcomes, targets, measures, and timelines; Lean methods to be used; data requirements; the scope of the project; and members of the team. Following sign-off, improvement events get underway.

Initiation is also when the organization should begin to develop its internal capacity by identifying internal Lean champions who can lead, drive, and deploy Lean as well as potential Lean leaders who will be trained to facilitate future events.

Lean Deployment Champions and Lean Leaders

All ministries within Canada's British Columbia and Saskatchewan governments have designated senior Lean Deployment Champions to lead, drive, and champion Lean implementation within their ministry and across the government. They are supported by middle manager Lean Leaders who have received specialized Lean training to facilitate events, support the implementation of continuous improvement plans, measure and track Lean outcomes, and assist executive leadership to build a culture of Lean within the ministry and government.

Lean Leader training is a process whereby, over time, Lean Leaders gain deeper understanding, skills, and experience with Lean methods. Ideally, they begin by observing an event or series of events – they *See*. Then they attend specialized Lean training oriented to facilitating Lean events, implementing improvements, and measuring results – they *Learn*. This is followed by co-facilitation of events and, ultimately, by independent facilitation – they *Do*. This approach recognizes the need for employees to gain confidence and experience using Lean over time. Lean facilitation can be very challenging because it requires that Lean Leaders question the status quo. This can include questioning managers within their organization who hold more senior positions than they do. Also, on occasion, someone will need to manage conflict, another skill that may have to be acquired over time.

The measuring, tracking, and celebrating of results also begins as the Lean process gets underway. It is critically important to capture and broadcast these improvements, both qualitative and quantitative, so they can be recognized and celebrated internally within the organization, and externally. This can be done in a variety of ways such as by posting "stories" of improvement on the intranet, internet, and newsletters; by hosting team recognition events; by visibly posting results in common areas; and, most importantly, by having executives visibly champion the initiative with employees who need to know Lean is achieving results to stay motivated and engaged.

The public is interested in knowing about improvements to public services, both from the perspective of the customer or user of the service, and from that of the citizen who is paying for it. For this same reason, governments are also interested in results so they can demonstrate value for the investment of public dollars in Lean.

At this stage in an organization's Lean journey, employees will perceive Lean as a series of Lean projects with continuous improvement plans that need implementing. Chances are they will be trying to "do" Lean in addition to everything they have always done – off the sides of their desk! As with any changes made in the workplace some employees will embrace Lean from the get-go, some will actively resist it, and others will fall somewhere in the middle.

Phase 4: Integration

The next phase in implementing Lean is integration which occurs when organizations begin to go beyond using Lean for transactional improvement to incorporating Lean as part of organizational transformation. This is the phase when departments and agencies begin to move from "doing Lean" to "being Lean" with Lean becoming part of the organizational culture.

At this point in an organization's Lean journey, leaders are becoming more strategic in the selection of value stream improvements. While tackling internal business processes, they are also beginning to identify ways to use Lean to assist them in improving core business and achieving their strategic plan. During phase 3 they are likely to shy from customer-facing Lean improvement, while in phase 4 they will be more comfortable taking on complex projects and engaging their customers to do so.

When Lean is being integrated into the heart of the organization, resources are being realigned to support improvement. Dedicated Lean Leaders are working with senior leaders to manage projects and assist with change management, data analysis, visual displays, communication, and recognition. Leaders are beginning to learn about Lean Management principles and disciplined efforts are underway to change leadership behaviors to focus more on engaging with staff, enhancing problem solving, mentoring and coaching, clarifying accountability relationships, recognizing success, and fostering culture change across the organization. (See Chapter 5 for more information about Lean Management.) Additionally, senior leaders may begin to explore use of *Hoshin Kanri* for strategic planning and deployment (Chapter 6).

As well as working within an organization, for example a state department, at this phase Lean may be expanded enterprise-wide to include all aspects of public service; for example, all departments of state government and its agencies. Forums may be created to improve internal processes such as recruitment, procurement, information technology, planning, and budgeting and to break down service silos across departments such as in human services, education, health, the environment, and the economy.

Phase 5: Sustainment

The final phase of the Lean journey is sustainment which occurs when an organization has fully embraced Lean philosophy and has incorporated Lean into the way it does business. *Hoshin Kanri* is likely used for strategic planning and deployment with citizens routinely involved in improvement activity. Lean leadership behaviors focus on leading with integrity and respect, and are practiced across the enterprise, with management regularly interacting with the frontline employees. Outcomes are measured, monitored, tracked, and reported; accountability is reinforced; and progress is celebrated. Continuous improvement is part of the culture of the organization. This can be seen in Figure 3-2, A Sustained Lean Enterprise.

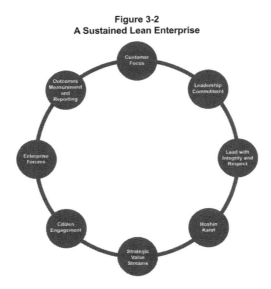

Deployment Trajectories

As organizations embark on their Lean journey they can expect interest, enthusiasm, and momentum to wax and wane over time. In our experience, sustaining Lean requires significant leadership commitment and the initiative will need to be refreshed and re-energized on a regular basis in order for an organization to move through the phases of implementation to sustain Lean. We can't emphasize enough the importance of "driving hard" to keep moving forward. Ideally, political leaders will publicly reinforce their continued commitment to Lean and will be involved in celebrating Lean improvement. At a minimum, executive leadership will need to be doing so and this may require an annual recommitment and refresh of the initiative. It is also advisable to put in place mechanisms to reinforce leadership accountability such as building Lean into the organization's performance management system and having leaders report on results to their peers.

The critical zone for commitment is around the end of the first year. As indicated in Figure 3-3, The Lean Trajectory,[2] ideally, organizations will follow trajectory A and make steady progress to sustaining Lean. In reality, they are more likely to experience their journey more along the lines of trajectory B.

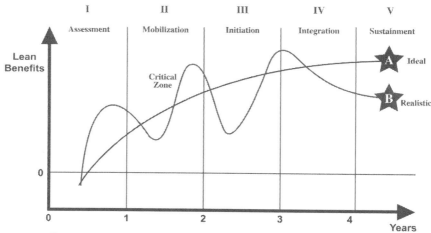

Figure 3-3 Lean Deployment Trajectories

- The objective is to sustain Lean which requires significant leadership commitment
- The critical zone is around the end of year one
- Commitment will wax and wane. There will be need to continually refresh

---

[2] Adapted from Smith and Blakeslee's 2002 book *Strategic Six Sigma: Best Practices from the Executive Suite*.

CASE STUDY
The United States National Institutes of Health (NIH) Lean Journey

Phase 1: Strategy and Assessment

The United States Department of Health and Human Services/National Institutes of Health (NIH) is dedicated to improving the health and wellness of all Americans, and is the largest biomedical research agency in the world. The agency has a thirty-three billion-dollar budget to support cutting-edge biomedical and clinical research aimed at discovering underlying causes of disease and translating scientific discoveries into effective interventions.

NIH began its Lean journey in November 2008, in its Office of Logistics and Acquisition Operations (OLAO). Leaders conducted an organizational assessment and recognized the need to find innovative methods to maintain productivity by using fewer resources. Like many public-sector organizations, the agency faced continual budget scrutiny and was expected to do more with less. NIH wanted to strengthen the efficiency and effectiveness of its business operations and knew this would require detailed and informative insight across the entire operation including staff, processes, controls, metrics, and technology.

NIH has twenty-seven distinct Institutes and Centers, each with its own research agenda and budget. The Institutes and Centers generally operate independently, with variety in how many similar processes are conducted. OLAO saw an opportunity to streamline processes across NIH while improving customer service and increasing the use of technology (that is, automation, dashboards, and reporting). It wanted a standardized approach for addressing scientific and administrative process inefficiencies across the agency. OLAO created a Lean Six Sigma (LSS) Program, an approach to process improvement oriented to removing the cause of efforts, defects, and variability in processes when rich numerical data is available. They focused on two primary components: training and project delivery.

Phase 2: Mobilization

NIH began by retaining external consulting expertise, which helped OLAO establish a Steering Committee and outline organizational goals and key performance indicators for the LSS program. The Steering Committee, comprised of OLAO division directors and branch chiefs, decided to pursue a standard training approach for LSS certification for employees. A one-day Executive Awareness training was developed for staffers who wanted to know the basics of Lean Six Sigma and potentially act in a Sponsor role for a project, along with a week-long LSS Green Belt course to equip employees for project delivery. The latter included building an LSS Certification Storyboard with guidance and templates to highlight criteria for consideration when certifying Green Belt candidates.

Phase 3: Initiation

The LSS Steering Committee, with assistance from the consultants, identified initial improvement opportunities that would move forward strategic business objectives and goals; it now reviews all proposed improvement projects. Green Belt candidates were selected and mentored by the consultants to lead improvement projects through use of the LSS process improvement framework DMAIC (Define, Measure, Analyze, Improve, and Control). The consultants provided operational project support while employees learned and adopted new processes and procedures. Project charters were developed identifying the business case, project goals, scope, and other details such as key stakeholders, including the project sponsors and process owners. Brown bag training sessions, weekly mentorship meetings with Green Belt candidates, and guidance for integrating LSS tools, methodologies, and approaches were provided. Leadership was kept engaged through direct involvement in projects, ad hoc project updates, and quarterly Steering Committee meetings.

**Figure 3-4
DMAIC Methodology and Phase Deliverables**

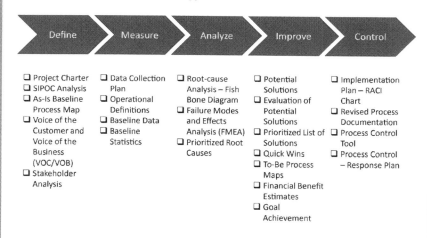

Phase 4: Integration

NIH has now expanded its LSS Program beyond the OLAO organization to support all of NIH and is in the process of integrating it within day-to-day business operations. The agency sees this as essential for identifying opportunities for ongoing improvement, as well as for achieving organizational and cultural change.

The program has trained more than three hundred employees in LSS, and has certified more than forty Green Belts. Improvement projects have ranged from reducing inventory overages and shortages to improving the monitoring of NIH's Grants Program, to increasing the number of scientific rodent cages washed per day. NIH is utilizing an integrated approach to verify improvement plans are implemented, key checkpoints and milestones are achieved, and there is continual alignment of LSS projects with overall strategic goals and objectives.

> *The part of my job I enjoy the most has to do with identifying ways to make things work more efficiently and the Lean Six Sigma approach will provide some wonderful tools....*
> — NIH Employee

While NIH leadership acknowledges that data collection and measurement has been challenging, NIH has found it to be extremely important to identify root causes and potential solutions. The agency is tracking measurable outcomes achieved using LSS tools (that is, process control mechanisms, control and response plans, escalation maps), and are witnessing qualitative benefits in the workplace achieved through coaching and mentorship. A cost-benefit analysis is completed for every improvement project. As of May 2016, NIH had achieved combined cost avoidance of forty-six million dollars, thanks to the implementation of Lean Six Sigma principles.

Phase 5: Sustainment

NIH is learning how to use continuous improvement on its own and plans to be self-sufficient and self-sustaining with Lean by December 2018. It has developed an improvement project "pipeline" aligned to strategy and linked to critical success factors and key performance indicators. The use of Lean is driving cultural change in the organization.

Following are some of the process improvement efforts that have been conducted across NIH.

DELIVERING RESULTS THAT MATTER

NIH Measurable Results

Improve Computer Package Refresh Process

- Streamlined the organization's operations, which reduced process lead time by 72 percent (from 247 hours to 70 hours)
- Decreased the number of staff working on the process by 69 percent (from thirteen to four)
- Reduced cost of process complexity by 74 percent (from 9,636 dollars to 2,516 dollars)
- Reduced surplus computer packages by 86.5 percent (from thirty-seven to five)
- Realized a cost avoidance of 7,000 dollars within the first year and an estimated 70,000 dollars over the next eight years

Acquisition Planning, Budgeting, & Reporting Improvement Initiative

- Realized 316,000 dollars in cost avoidance from a 50 percent reduction in budget adjustments
- Realized 48,000 dollars in cost avoidance from a 50 percent reduction in account number changes

Third-Party Storage Project

- Reduced property accountability process cost by 90 percent (from 9,089 dollars to 909 dollars)
- Realized a cost avoidance of 8,000 dollars in the first year
- Increased inventory accuracy rate to 100 percent for accountable assets

IT Contractor Invoicing Improvement Initiative

- Reduced the number of incorrectly submitted invoices by 100 percent
- Reduced the time it took to review and submit payment for all IT Contractor invoices by 50% (from sixty days to thirty days

Property Overage Reduction Initiative

- Identified a potential increase in revenue of 109,500 dollars
- Increased revenue from October_December 2012 by 26,500 dollars

Shortage Identification & Mitigation Initiative

- Found 6,552 items, identified as Shortages, accounting for 27.4 million dollars in assets

Improve Inventory Metrics Reporting

- Reduced process lead time by 99.5 percent (from 320 hours to 1.5 hours annually)
- Automated NIH metric generation process, which increased metric set accuracy by eliminating 99 percent of human errors and standardized metric reports 100 percent of the time
- Reduced person-hours by 99.5 percent resulting in a cost avoidance of 13,200 dollars the first year and an estimated 85,100 dollars over the next six years

Improve Supply Center Replenishment Process

- Reduced Replenishment Lead Time (RLT) by an average of 11 percent (from an average of 24.6 days to 22 days)
- Reduced acquisition cycle time by 11 percent (from an average of nine days to eight days)
- Reduced process lead time for micro-purchases by 27 percent (from an average of fifteen days to eleven days)
- Reduced zero balance by 71.5 percent (from 20 percent to 5.7 percent)
- Achieved an average cost reduction per contract action of 37.65 dollars, resulting in a total cost avoidance of 534,600 dollars in the first year and 1.66 million dollars over the next three years

Lab Grade (LG) Freezer Accountability Project

- Increased LG freezer accountability from 68 percent to 93 percent
- Combined financial benefits of 10 million dollars in the first year and 30 million dollars over the next three years

Improve Rodent Cage Handling Process

- Eliminated dirty cages by 91 percent, from an average of 1,393 dirty cage components left unwashed at the end of the day (October_December) to an average of 127 dirty cage components left unwashed at the end of the day (March_May). June data reflects a 100 percent reduction in leftover cage components.
- Achieved a cost avoidance of 66,700 dollars annually, by discontinuing the use of an inefficient machine
- Created a performance-based contract with a service provider to keep machines >70 percent operational, resulting in the organization potentially receiving a credit of up to ten thousand dollars annually for underperformance

Chapter 4

GOVERNANCE AND OVERSIGHT

Implementing large-scale change is challenging for any organization. This is especially true for public-sector organizations that are constrained by political and bureaucratic hierarchies, complex legislative and regulatory requirements, a risk adverse public service, outdated technology, and the generally accepted public and political expectations of being able to "do more with less."

While change is challenging for any organization, for the public sector it is imperative because there is a public expectation that services can and should be more effective, efficient, safe, and responsive. We believe Lean is ideal for bringing about change by improving performance while controlling costs. Implementing Lean is in the public interest since it can lead to refreshed, renewed, innovative, and revitalized public services. It can also break down traditional silos within governments and strengthen services enterprise-wide.

Basic change theory dictates that all organizations embarking on a change agenda can expect some people within the organization to be early adapters, some to be active resisters, and many to be in the middle adopting a "wait and see" attitude. This is true for individuals at all levels of an organization, from the frontline to executive management and, in the public sector, amongst the elected as well.

Public-sector organizations can expect energy and enthusiasm for Lean to ebb and wane, depending on what phase of implementation they are in and where they are at in terms of their Lean trajectory (see Chapter 3). There will be both successes and challenges along the way. When leading with Lean, many factors need to be considered and, indeed, they are crucial for minimizing risk and ensuring successful implementation.

Leadership

Lean implementation starts with an acknowledgment by senior leaders that there are significant organizational problems which cannot be adequately addressed by traditional approaches. They understand that the status quo is not acceptable and that change is required. Lean is adopted as the approach to be used to bring about the necessary changes and improvements.

But, how do senior leaders become aware of the potential of Lean in the first place? How do they gain knowledge and understanding of what Lean is and how it works? In short, someone at the executive level needs to be a visionary to bring Lean to the table. Without executive leadership, Lean is unlikely to move beyond project-based process improvement and the full benefit of Lean management will not be realized.

In our work, we have consistently encountered mid-level public service employees who use Lean methods on Lean process improvement projects, but are frustrated by a lack of knowledge or interest in Lean by executive management. They know leadership support is required to fully reap the benefits of Lean and help the organization move forward on its strategic plan. The senior team needs to understand Lean and its potential, commit to implementation, and put in place the necessary mechanisms for sustaining the initiative. This includes setting aside time to be trained, engage, coach, and mentor staff, enhance problem solving, clarify accountability relationships, recognize success, and foster culture change across the organization. This allows an organization to move beyond "doing" Lean to "being" Lean and successfully progress through the stages of Lean implementation.

Governance

We recommend putting in place a robust governance structure at several levels within the organization to oversee Lean implementation and ensure the initiative is sustained. The configuration of governance will depend on the nature of the organization but, regardless, we recommend dedicated executive-level steering committees, appointment of senior leaders to act as champions for the initiative, dedicated teams to oversee Lean operations, and the recruitment or training of Lean Leaders.

Lean Steering Committee

The Lean Steering Committee oversees all aspects of Lean implementation and monitors continuous improvement across the organization on an ongoing basis. Especially in the early stages, we recommend a dedicated Lean senior-level committee since considerable time is required to plan, secure resources, communicate, monitor, problem solve, and remove obstacles to success. Depending on the size of the organization, it may also be prudent to establish working-level subcommittees or department/branch committees to promote and support the initiative.

Lean Office

For large public-sector organizations, establishment of a small Lean Office to manage deployment under direction of the Lean Steering Committee is advantageous. For example, the Lean Office in British Columbia and New Brunswick's Office of Strategy Management each have a staff of only about ten individuals who manage deployment across government departments. The Lean Office provides a coordination function for deployment across the enterprise and works with individual departments, ministries, or branches to secure resources, coordinate training, track progress, and measure results. The Lean Office also manages the consulting contract, if applicable, and may act as the administrative arm to the Lean Steering Committee by organizing meetings, developing agendas, taking minutes, tracking progress, and so on.

Lean Deployment Champions

We suggest Lean Deployment Champions be appointed by senior leadership to promote and drive Lean within a department, ministry, city, agency, or publicly funded institution. They are responsible for establishing local governance structures within their area of the organization, and for developing their internal Lean deployment strategy including selection of improvement events and targets, employee engagement approach, training plans, communications, and so on. Deployment Champions should report to the most senior manager; for example, the deputy minister, city manager, CEO, or president.

Lean Leaders

Depending on the size of the organization, several Lean Leaders will need to be recruited or trained to help deploy the initiative. Lean Leaders work under the direction of the Lean Deployment Champion to facilitate and lead teams through Lean events, deliver employee Lean orientations, monitor progress in implementing continuous improvement plans, measure and track quantitative and qualitative outcomes, prepare visibility walls and displays, and provide general advice aimed at creating and sustaining a culture of Lean. These are skilled individuals with expertise who will be in demand both internally and externally. Organizations need to make every effort to retain their skilled Lean Leaders while anticipating some turnover as, inevitably, a few will be poached by other organizations.

> Lean Leaders in New Brunswick, called Process Improvement Facilitators, are Certified Lean Six Sigma Black Belts. They are dedicated full-time to driving improvement to ensure they are not distracted by day-to-day operational crises.

Engaging the Board and Elected Representatives

The role of the public service is to implement policy in accordance with government direction. As such, Lean implementation and the management of continuous improvement is generally the purview of the public service. But the results of Lean, the outcomes, are of significant interest to the board of directors, if applicable, and elected representatives who are inherently interested in improving services for constituents and increasing the value of public investment.

Politicians can be strong advocates for Lean and can play an important role in generating interest among employee and stakeholder groups, and in communicating results to the general public. In some jurisdictions, government leaders have publicly embraced Lean as a means of achieving government direction. For example, the governor of the state of Washington and the mayor of the city of Denver are robust champions, consistently referencing outcomes achieved in public communications, and are actively involved in leading with Lean.

Usually, interest in Lean emerges from within a public sector organization and is brought to the board and political levels for information and support. Despite its benefits, governments and boards can be wary about Lean because it requires public-sector organizations to be transparent about their problems. Some find it difficult to be open about issues such as waiting times for surgery, workplace injuries, infection rates, and so on. Lean makes problems such as these transparent, along with measurable improvement or the lack of it. Governments are also accountable for any investment of public dollars, including those made to implement Lean. Therefore, it would be prudent for senior officials to educate and inform their boards and political leaders about Lean early in their Lean journey. Ideally, this would include an orientation to Lean thinking so board and elected representatives could not only support implementation, but also apply Lean principles to improve their own processes (for example, board governance and decision-making relating to budgets).

It may also be important for governments to publicly demonstrate the benefits they are realizing as a result of their investment in Lean and it is the responsibility of the public service to provide the necessary information for the government to do so. We can't highlight enough the importance of measuring and communicating the investment made and the benefits realized including qualitative service delivery improvements and safety enhancements, as well as quantitative measures such as cost savings, cost avoidance, and productivity enhancements. Citizens have the right to know that public dollars being invested in Lean are paying off in terms of safer, better, and more efficient public services.

CASE STUDY
Government of Saskatchewan, Canada

The Province of Saskatchewan began its Lean journey in 2006 with a pilot project in File Hills Health Region. It was such a success that all regional health authorities in the province adopted Lean in 2009. All government ministries adopted Lean in 2010. Also, in 2012-13, some school divisions and all the major post-secondary institutions began implementing Lean. The extensive commitment to Lean across government, in its publicly funded institutions and in government-operated business, makes Saskatchewan a Canadian leader in public sector Lean implementation.

The Challenge

Prior to embarking on their Lean journey, health regions, school divisions, post-secondary institutions, and government ministries primarily operated in isolation from one another. A variety of methodologies and approaches to leadership, management, and process improvement were utilized with consulting expertise engaged on an ad hoc basis as required. At the same time, there was increasing recognition of the need to engage citizens and employees to renew public services to improve quality, efficiency, safety, transparency, and accountability. CEOs and deputy ministers recognized the potential benefits of adopting Lean, including the impact it could have on strengthening the culture of the public service, and they decided to move forward with implementation. Two separate initiatives were undertaken: one across the health sector and the second across all government ministries along with select school divisions and post-secondary institutions.

The Approach

Similar approaches were used in healthcare and in government (including school divisions and post-secondary institutions). Implementation in healthcare was overseen by health region CEOs and, in government, by a committee of deputy ministers. Participation was made mandatory for both sectors (although not for school divisions and post-secondary institutions which were, instead, "expected" to use Lean). Ministers were engaged, Requests for Proposals (RFPs) issued, and external consultants procured to provide support for implementation. Training began with an initial focus on building senior executive knowledge, leadership, and support. It was then extended to others in management and made available to frontline employees. Specialized Lean Leader training was also provided to build internal expertise and the capacity, over time, to conduct Lean improvement independently without the use of consultants. Lean Deployment Champions were identified within each organization to drive the initiative. Small Lean offices were established in each health region and in the Ministry of Health (this function was subsequently moved into the Health Quality Council). A modest Lean office was also established to provide central oversight within government. Job descriptions were built and existing quality improvement positions were converted into dedicated Lean positions with a common mandate and approach. A standard format for measuring and reporting improvement was put in place so results could be documented and rolled-up for the benefit of the government.

By the end of the 2014-15 fiscal year, both the health sector and government had ended their consulting contracts and were using internal resources for improvement. Also, the government had named a Minister and Deputy Minister Responsible for Lean. Despite these steps, sustaining Lean implementation continued to be a significant challenge, particularly in light of criticism from the major opposing political party and the media.

In Saskatchewan, the government's use of consultants, along with the associated costs, has always been a subject of scrutiny by the major opposing party, media, and the public. The health sector's major Lean contract was originally for fifty million dollars over five years (thirty-nine million dollars was actually spent). While this is a modest sum when compared to 5.6 billion dollars in annual spending for health in the province, it was still a substantial investment. While initial implementation was supported by health practitioners including physicians and nurses, not unlike with any major change initiative, there were some naysayers. Unfortunately, provider groups expressed concern about cost, the number of staff involved, the pace of implementation, bullying from consultants, and questioning the relevance of a private sector approach to publicly delivered healthcare. They also indicated a "cult" mentality was emerging among leaders as evidenced by the extensive use of Japanese Lean terminology. The major opposition party made little effort to understand Lean and was quick to recognize a political opportunity. It made Lean in healthcare an almost daily issue in the legislature and the media responded with extensive coverage. Government responded defensively by attempting to profile results achieved, but, for whatever reason, failed to go on the offense in support for the initiative.

A more modest sum of five million dollars over five years was spent on consulting for Lean implementation in government ministries, school divisions, and post-secondary institutions. While public criticism in these sectors was minimal, the fact that Lean in healthcare has been so prominent in the Legislative Assembly and in the news has led to significant challenges to sustaining the interest and enthusiasm for Lean at both political and executive levels. As a result, since 2013_2014 there has been a significant decline in Lean improvement activity across all sectors and the province is no longer seeing the same level of results that were achieved in the early years of implementation.

These mixed results point to the importance of a clearly developed implementation plan as well as the need for ongoing engagement and communication at all levels. Lean is worth it! In the public sector, service providers can dominate and the unions can be strong. They must be engaged and brought on as supporters from the very beginning. They need to understand how they can benefit and be a part of improvement efforts _ especially since reducing waste and increasing efficiency may run counter to their best interests as, for example, it does when overtime is reduced. For the most part, public servants want to do the right thing for their customer, patient, student, or client. They want to make a difference by adding value for their customer. Their jobs are more rewarding when they are operating efficiently and spending time focused on value-added activity. Being a part of making things better is rewarding in and of itself.

Engaging clients and stakeholders is also critical to building support and, as a general rule, a modest approach to implementation is best. There should be just enough funding to build momentum; also, leaders driving the initiative with integrity and respect, and training that generates understanding and commitment but is not so rigorous as to interfere with the core business of leaders, managers, and employees. The Lean process should be strategically targeted to improving outcomes that matter.

The Results

The Government of Saskatchewan has invested fifty million dollars since 2010 in Lean (forty-five million dollars in health and five million dollars in government ministries, school divisions, and post-secondary institutions). As of July 2016, there were more than 2,300 public sector Lean improvement initiatives with 1,350+ in health, 800+ in ministries, 130+ in school divisions, and 100+ in post-secondary institutions. Together, these improvements have led to about 172 million dollars in cost savings/avoidance including 140 million dollars in the health sector and another 32 million dollars in ministries, school divisions, and post-secondary institutions (Government of Saskatchewan, July 2016).

But the real benefits of Lean are the tangible improvements which are having a positive impact on the citizens of the province such as reductions in surgical wait times, shorter student registration waiting times for international students entering Saskatchewan Polytechnic, shorter lineups, less paperwork and faster bank deposits for student loans, significant reductions in waiting for children in school needing to see a psychologist or requiring speech language support, and quicker turnaround for industry seeking approval to drill horizontal wells.

The Future

Saskatchewan has now replaced references to "Lean" with "continuous improvement" and there is no longer a position with the title of "Minister" or "Deputy Minister" Responsible for Lean. While there appears to be continuing support in the healthcare sector, and government ministries indicate they continue to be committed to the initiative, only time will tell if there will be sufficient leadership support at political and executive levels to sustain Saskatchewan's Lean journey into the future.

"Push" versus "Pull" Participation

Depending on the nature of the public-sector organization, it will be important at the start for the leadership to determine what approach it wishes to take to initiate Lean. Some jurisdictions have mandated participation with every division and branch of government expected to participate, with the performance of leadership assessed accordingly. Others, like Manitoba, started with pilot projects. New Brunswick took a "pull" approach by inviting deputy ministers to compete to be selected as a pilot group of six departments. This approach was then expanded to other departments and, on a voluntary basis, to interested regional health authority and education districts (Washburn, Summer 2014).

Training

In our view, over time, every person within an organization that is implementing Lean should gain some level of familiarity with Lean philosophy and methods. This can be accomplished through a variety of approaches including employee orientation, online training, traditional classroom learning, and/or active participation in Lean events.

Because leadership is so important to successful implementation, we recommend beginning with training those at the top, in executive management. Training can then be cascaded to other managers, supervisors, and employees throughout the organization.

There are numerous approaches which can be used for Lean training related to content, delivery, hours, certification, and so on. When mobilizing, a public-sector organization will need to do a careful assessment of its training requirements and capacity. There are options to develop and deliver training internally, purchase it from a private vendor, or use a combination of public and private-sector delivery. For example, the Government of British Columbia and the City of Denver have developed and are delivering their own introductory and Lean Leader training. Saskatchewan initially procured training from private consultants and then moved on to deliver training in-house. New Brunswick has Six Sigma-trained employees who are training their own staff.

The nature of the training itself varies extensively from simple orientation and one-day introductory training to three- or five-day Lean Leader training to Six Sigma yellow, green, black, and master black belt training, which can take up to twenty days. In Saskatchewan's healthcare system, Lean certification requires eighty days of training and includes extensive hands-on participation in Rapid Process Improvement activity.

Resource Allocation

The effort required to implement Lean and the necessary financial and people resources depends on the size and complexity of the organization. Lean budgets typically contain dedicated funds for training, facilitation, generalized consulting support, and establishment of a modest Lean office. Most organizations secure initial support from the private sector following issuance of a Request for Proposals (RFP) with the intention of weaning themselves from external assistance over time. Ideally, the necessary funds can be reallocated from other sources within the public service agency, especially if it can demonstrate benefits for the investment shortly following implementation.

For larger public-sector organizations, we recommend dedicated Lean Leaders be trained to support Lean Deployment Champions and executive management throughout their Lean journey. Many jurisdictions have Lean Leaders trying to do Lean "off the sides of their desk" and they struggle to prioritize continuous improvement work over other operational issues and crises. Lean resources can be shared across branches or departments. Not only is this efficient, it also helps break down silos within an organization and can lead to identification of corporate or enterprise-wide Lean initiatives.

Enterprise Lean Forums

Lean can help an organization change for the better by improving programs, services, and processes but the Lean journey, in and of itself, is a change process and, as with any significant change effort, mechanisms need to be put in place to support change agents and other employees within the organization. For this reason, we recommend creation of a number of enterprise forums, especially for larger organizations. These can mirror the agency's Lean governance structure and should, at a minimum, include forums for executive management, Lean Deployment Champions, and Lean Leaders.

Enterprise Lean forums can be a key mechanism for problem solving, group learning, sharing ideas, communicating results, and creating common tools and approaches for application across the Lean organization. Periodically, an organization may also want to consider organizing events for managers and supervisors and/or frontline employees to help inform staff, generate buzz, and celebrate success.

Measuring Results

To lead with Lean, senior leaders need to know how they are doing with respect to implementation. Are they achieving results? Are internal and external processes, programs, and services safer, improved, and more efficient? Are Lean improvement events occurring within departments and across the enterprise, and are continuous improvement plans being implemented? Are managers, supervisors, employees, and stakeholders adjusting to Lean as the new way of doing business?

Governments around the world, without exception, struggle to measure and report outcomes. This is particularly true for "soft" public services such as education, health, and social services. It is very difficult to measure the impact of a particular intervention on the well-being of a population. Having said this, we can't emphasize enough the importance of monitoring, measuring, and reporting on results. At the end of the day, results including those related to efficiency, service delivery improvement, and broader outcomes in health, education, and the economy are what matter.

Lean organizations know that *what gets measured is what gets done*. It is critical for public service organizations to put systems in place to capture, drive, and maintain the improvements sought within the organization. It's also important, as much as possible, for this information to be current so adjustments can be made if the data shows the organization is not moving in the right direction. In Saskatchewan, for example, efforts are underway to improve graduation rates and the literature is clear that grade 3 reading levels are a predictor of success. For this reason, school divisions are focusing effort in this area and there has been an improvement from 65 percent of students reading at grade level in 2013 to 74 percent in 2016 (CBC Saskatchewan, 2016). This, officials expect, will impact graduation rates in the future.

To begin, public-sector organizations need to develop a set of outcome measures, followed by a variety of process and activity metrics that provide an indication of what's happening with respect to the outcomes. This is not easy, but public-sector organizations are accountable to the public and they must be able to demonstrate improvement. For this reason, it is necessary to capture a variety of quantitative and qualitative information about service, cost, effort, and quality. Once the outcomes are known and metrics established, it is then possible to determine baselines and targets for improvement. The Lean office can play a key support role here by designing metrics, scorecards, and visual displays to capture Lean activity and results from across the organization.

Tracking Lean activity and outcomes is important at both the macro and micro levels of an organization. Leaders define the outcomes they wish to achieve and monitor overall progress. Managers and supervisors put in place and monitor processes and activities in support of organizational outcomes. Employees do the most important work, on the floor. At all levels, measurement and reporting is required to monitor progress, make needed adjustments, and determine results. The best data is relevant, clear, easy to understand, detailed enough to inform future action, robust enough to allow for trend identification, accepted, and accurate. In our experience, there are often reams of data available to public-sector organizations. The challenge is often extracting the information and having the resources and expertise to analyze it.

When data is available, fact-based decision-making can occur. Where necessary, corrective action plans can be put in place to ensure continued momentum and sustainment of the initiative. Results can be shared and success celebrated.

CASE STUDY
Washington State Department of Corrections

The Washington State Department of Corrections manages all state-operated adult prisons and supervises adults who live in the community. According to its 2017-2021 Strategic Plan, the department's mission is "to improve public safety." Its commitment is "to operate a safe and humane corrections system and partner with others to transform lives for a better Washington." The plan outlines five goals as follows:

- Engaged and Respected Employees
- Safer Operations
- Innovative, Efficient, and Sustainable Business Practices
- Supporting Successful Transition
- Promoting Positive Change (Washington State Institute for Public Policy, December 2014)

The Challenge

Establishing clear goals and priorities, setting targets, developing action plans, and assessing performance is a significant challenge for any public-sector organization because of competing priorities, lack of data, challenges with measurement, and wariness about openness, transparency, and public accountability. Results Washington is a leader in this regard. It is the State's data-driven initiative aimed at making government more effective, efficient, and customer-focused. Launched in 2013, Results Washington is helping drive improvements on dozens of key goals and is using Lean to deliver on the governor's priorities. (For more information see Chapter 5, which includes a Results Washington case study.) The State Department of Corrections is part of the Results Washington initiative and is committed to delivering results for the benefit of Washingtonians.

The Approach

A top-down, bottom-up process is in place to ensure alignment of the governor's strategic priorities with the work of the State Department of Corrections. Results Washington and the department have worked together to identify the following outcome measures related to Corrections as part of achieving the Results Washington goal of Safe and Healthy Communities. These include:

- Decrease rate of return to institutions from 27.8 percent to 25 percent by 2020
- Increase percentage of individuals complying with their conditions of supervision of case plan from 75 percent to 78 percent by 2017

- Increase percentage of adults who are employed post-release from 30 percent to 40 percent by 2017; and
- Decrease rate of violent infractions in prison from 1.0 to 0.90 per 100 incarcerated individuals by 2017

To translate the governor's high-level priorities into actions which will help move the needle, the Department of Corrections has cascaded these throughout the department and into its correctional facilities and field offices. Lean problem solving and root cause analysis is in constant use at all levels, and a variety of action plans (using the standard A3 approach adopted by the governor's office) are in place from the management level down to the frontline and shop floor. Action plans within Correctional Industries' (CI) furniture manufacturing plant at the Strafford Creek Corrections Center, for example, prioritize the achievement of marketable skills among the incarcerated population so they can be successfully employed upon release. Similarly, Lean improvements carried out on the shop floor are providing inmates with direct experience in Lean and are increasing safety and reducing the cost of equipment and materials. (For more information see Chapter 2, which includes a case study on Washington State Correctional Industries.) Progress is monitored, results are measured, action plans are adjusted, reports are developed, and results are "rolled-up" to Results Washington.

Interesting as well are efforts being made within the department to contribute to the governor's broader priorities beyond corrections. The sustainability program at the Washington Corrections Center for Women includes a horticulture program, facility gardens, conservation program, food composing, and recycling _ all oriented to increasing sustainability and environmental awareness.

> *Correctional Industries' commitment to building sustainability in all its business operations includes environmentally friendly and recycled material for manufacturing, creating products that can be completely recycled, offering recycling services, and developing zero-waste processes. But it also includes trimming down our procedures and processes to avoid needless delays, repetitive efforts, waste, and unnecessary manpower* (Washington State Department of Corrections, 2016).

The Results

Washington State's Department of Corrections is successfully using Lean thinking and approaches to translate the governor's priorities into actions from a strategic level to a tactical level at the frontline and in CI shops.

There is alignment from the level of the elected representatives, executive management, frontline employees, and even inmates.

As the following data shows, because the department has clear targets and measures, it recognizes it needs to make more progress to meet targets with respect to recidivism and compliance with supervision of case plans; however, it also shows that the agency is making considerable progress regarding post-release employment and the rate of violent infractions in prison:

- As of December 2016, the rate of return to institutions for offenders was 32.2 percent, short of the 25.0 percent target by 2020.
- As of November 2016, the percentage of offenders complying with conditions of supervision was 74 percent, short of the 78 percent target by 2017.
- At the end of the third quarter of 2016, the percentage of adults employed post-release was 38.4 percent, short of the 40 percent target but substantially higher than the 30 percent baseline.
- As of September 2016, the rate of violent infractions in prison was .81 percent per one hundred incarcerated individuals below the 0.90 target by 2017.

The department is also tracking other contributions it is making to the state economy. For example, a benefit-cost estimate conducted in 2014 concluded 4.77 dollars is saved in future criminal justice costs in relation to each dollar spent on CI programs due to a reduction in recidivism (Washington State Institute for Public Policy, 2014). Additionally, purchases from local suppliers and staff salaries contribute about 38.8 million dollars to the state economy (Washington State Department of Corrections, 2016). The department is also monitoring market share to ensure it grows in-prison employment opportunities without adversely affecting the private sector. (Of CI's nineteen operations, sixteen have a market share of less than 2 percent, three have a market share of less than 3 percent, and CI is the only in-state manufacturer for two operations, license plates and validation tabs.)

The Future

As part of its commitment to continuous improvement, the Department of Corrections will make ongoing adjustments to its action plans in support of the governor's priorities. It will "Plan," "Do," "Check," and Adjust" as required to achieve better results for the benefit of all Washingtonians.

Public Sector Lean Accountability

When implementing Lean, public-sector organizations also need to measure the impact of the Lean initiative itself. They are accountable for their Lean investment and need to ensure they are in a position to justify it to government and the public. For example, in Saskatchewan, the Provincial Auditor has undertaken two reviews of Lean implementation, one in healthcare and the second in executive government. In the most recent review the auditors recommended that those responsible for the Lean initiative set measures to enable assessment of its overall success, and set targets for key measures related to the use of Lean (Provincial Auditor of Saskatchewan, 2015).

To measure the results of their Lean initiative, public-sector organizations need to capture quantitative and qualitative information pertaining to individual Lean improvement events including service improvements, cost savings, costs avoided, and efficiency gains. Quantitative data can then be "rolled up" across the organization and combined with qualitative "stories" of improvement to illustrate the benefits of Lean.

Measuring Lean Implementation

For executive leaders, it is also important to be able to monitor the progress of the Lean implementation process itself – that is, how Lean is being incorporated into the culture of the organization. Again, this requires establishment of a variety of measures. We have found it to be helpful for an organization to survey employees, stakeholders, and the public about their knowledge, attitudes, and experience with Lean. This should be done early in the implementation process to establish a baseline and annually thereafter to monitor change. For example, the following brief questions can tell leaders a great deal about employee beliefs about Lean.

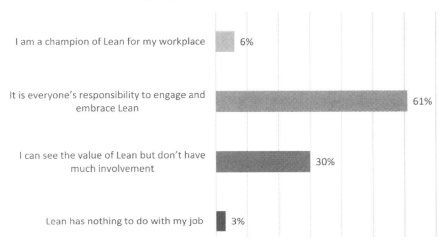

Employee Beliefs About Lean

Other measures to consider include number of completed Lean events, number of planned events, status of implementation of continuous improvement plans, number of citizen-facing or external events versus number of internal events, number of events with customer involvement, and so on. Several years following implementation, an organization may also wish to consider conducting a formal maturity assessment to determine how embedded Lean is within the culture of the organization.

Reporting Progress and Communicating Results

Once an organization has measures in place and begins monitoring results, we advocate making them visible to employees, customers, stakeholders, and the public so everyone can celebrate the progress and contribute to continuous improvement. By preparing a robust internal and external communications strategy, organizations can be strategic about their communications approach and employ a variety of communication mechanisms such as news releases, websites, intranet, social media, visual displays, electronic newsletters, member statements, Lean tours, speaking engagements, and so on.

Storytelling can be invaluable in communicating results in a way that reaches the hearts and minds of both internal and external audiences. Lean can have a significant impact on clients and employees. Helping them to tell their stories validates experience and can be of particular benefit to sustaining momentum for the organization's Lean journey. The City of Denver, for example, creates impact statements called "bright spots" to highlight improvement innovations (Elms, 2016).

Communicating results internally is critical to achieving buy-in and support for the initiative. This is essential to ensuring employee engagement and is an important means for celebrating success. Handled well, internal communications show frontline staff what Lean is and how they can play a direct role in improving service for their customer. By seeing the results of Lean efforts underway across an organization, employee enthusiasm can be generated, ideas for further improvement identified, and a culture of continuous improvement created.

It is also important to communicate the results of improvement efforts externally. The public wants to know public-sector dollars are being spent in appropriate ways that are beneficial to citizens. Ideally, two-way communication mechanisms can be put in place so citizens can provide comments and suggestions about what they think is important, and how they believe programs and service should be transformed. The public-sector organization should respond and be proactive in reaching out to citizens on topics that matter.

A variety of states in the U.S. are being very transparent about improvements they have made and the results they are achieving. This goes beyond communication of large-scale accomplishments to include smaller gains being achieved as a result of Lean.

Results Washington, http://www.results.wa.gov/, is an example of open government. It indicates it is committed to *building a more responsive, data-driven state government to get results*. Its website profiles the state's major strategic and operational priorities, and progress being made on achieving their goals. The focus is on results, although the website also provides information and resources on Lean as it is a key strategy they are using to *create a culture that encourages respect, creativity and innovative problem solving, continuously improves and eliminates waste from government processes, aligns efforts across state agencies and delivers results that matter to Washingtonians* (Washington State).

Lean Ohio, http://lean.ohio.gov/ focuses on results being achieved across the state and features "stories" along with a variety of information, education and learning items (Ohio State n.d.).

Minnesota's Office for Continuous Improvement, http://mn.gov/admin/lean/, has a results link which profiles success stories, agency results, as well as projects and events underway that are aimed at *better government and improved outcomes* (Minnesota State).

Results Iowa, Iowa http://www.resultsiowa.org/, provides information on the state's leadership agenda (priorities), economic indicators, and performance of departments. Measures and progress are emphasized using "at a glance" graphs which are easy to read and understand (Iowa State n.d.).

Get Lean Florida, http://www.getleanflorida.com/, provides an opportunity for citizens to communicate with the state's Chief Financial Officer about *how state government can better serve, including ideas for eliminating fraud, waste, and abuse or for improving how state government operates* (Florida State).

CASE STUDY
A Canadian Province's Ministry of Transportation

By Craig Szelestowski,
Head of Lean Agility's Lean Government Practice

The Challenge

A Canadian province's Ministry of Transportation granted renewals of permits for businesses to operate commercial vehicles. They had a backlog of more than four thousand files with a client waiting period of more than ninety days. Employees were stressed and clients, anxious to keep their businesses running, made thirty to forty progress-chasing calls a day. One of the causes of the backlog was a twice a year variation in demand for permits during high seasons: April, when landscaping companies prepare their trucks for the new season, and September, when snow-clearing companies do the same. Try as they might, employees in the renewals process could not deal with these spikes in demand. Backlogs accumulated and employees were unable to reduce them before the next peak month hit, creating a chronic backlog.

The Strategy

Backlogs can spiral when there is variation in incoming client demand or an inadequate supply of staff to do the work. A public employee within the ministry who had been trained in Lean facilitation worked with his Lean coach to examine ministry legislation and processes. It was determined that by renewing permits at the same time as vehicle registration, demand could be distributed more evenly over the course of the year, reducing staff inundation (from volume of permits and progress-chasing calls from clients). Cross-training staff from other units to increase capacity during peak periods further reduced inundation. As well, rework created by client-unfriendly forms reduced follow-up calls, freeing more capacity. Making the process visible with whiteboards and holding regular stand-up improvement meetings allowed them to continue to improve as a normal part of their daily work.

DELIVERING RESULTS THAT MATTER

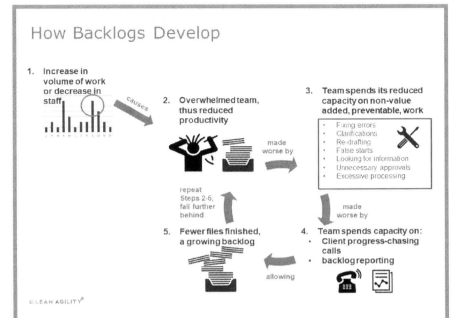

The Results

Three years and several peak periods later, the team in the permit renewal process still delivers renewals in three to five days, and the backlog has not returned. They were so inspired by their success that they also found the capacity to eliminate a backlog of more than one thousand files in a second process, reducing the waiting time for a permit for a first-time applicant from one month to a single day. This was done without investing in technology, headcount, or by working harder.

The Future

Ministry employees learned that to be sustainable, a one-time process improvement is not enough to eliminate a backlog forever. Without continuous improvement, backlogs can easily return. They know that processes, like nature, are subject to entropy _ it takes energy and good habits to maintain a high level of performance or else performance regresses to mediocrity, or chaos.

Chapter 5

LEADING, MANAGING, AND STRATEGIC USE OF LEAN

Lean is a business philosophy that focuses on transactional improvement at the operational level as well as transformational change in strategy, management, processes, culture, and systems to achieve and sustain maximum performance. As an organization gains experience with Lean, it will begin to shift from a culture of "doing" Lean to "being" Lean. When this occurs, employees identify Lean as more than a series of improvement projects and understand that it is, in fact, the way they do business. This juncture – where Lean leadership and management are instrumental for the organization – marks the next step in the Lean journey.

What Is Lean Management?

Lean Management is a structured methodology with a set of beliefs, concrete practices, and tools. It is intended to unite the organization's staff and processes to support organizational goals and objectives. Lean Management equips frontline supervisors, managers, and executive leaders with skills and tools to manage more effectively and foster a culture of continuous improvement.

To sustain Lean implementation, an organization may need to change the way it has approached leadership, management, and supervision. Lean organizations, first and foremost, emphasize customer service. They engage customers and employees to improve all types of services, enhance safety, and become more efficient. Managers are more present "on the floor" interacting with employees to remove barriers to improvement. Lean Management requires that an organization empower employees to solve problems they encounter in their everyday positions. The work of the organization is also organized and managed in accordance with its value streams – the start-to-finish process or steps that organizations take to deliver a product, service, or experience to its customer.

Management in Lean organizations operates from both top-down and bottom-up. Executive management provides overall directions, but also engages and confers with middle managers and employees who understand the day-to-day work of the organization best. Together, these employees bring together data from across the organization to track progress and manage performance.

Lean managers reinforce a culture of continuous improvement by listening to the customer and engaging with staff through teaching, training, and mentoring, and by encouraging innovation. Managers know that to make improvement, organizations need to be able to accept some level of risk and that people may make mistakes and initiatives fail. Lean managers accept this reality as part of doing business, but they put in place mechanisms to monitor initiatives so they can recognize early on when something isn't working and take corrective action.

Principal Elements of Lean Management

The following elements of Lean Management, when used together, can ensure improvement is achieved and sustained:

- Aligning teams to focus on organizational goals including defining key metrics to monitor progress to attainment of the goals
- Improving the visibility of performance through use of visual controls and visibility walls or information centers
- Arranging consistent daily operational meetings or "huddles" to help teams assess performance, drive accountability, and improve teamwork
- Coaching on problem-solving techniques and the use of structured project management (A3s) to enhance performance and provide staff with the tools they need to solve problems in their daily work
- Putting in place processes to monitor progress, identify needed corrective action, and sustain the work

- Driving culture change by embedding values and practice in the daily routines of managers and supervisors
- Coaching and mentoring employees to achieve results
- Motivating staff through employee recognition and by celebrating success

Understanding the elements of Lean Management is only the first step. The real challenge organizations face is putting them into practice and executing them effectively. This is a significant undertaking that requires training, coaching, and capacity building within the organization. We believe adoption of a structured, disciplined approach to implementing a Lean Management System is ideal. But before discussing this further, it is useful to explain some common Lean Management concepts including leader standard work, visual controls, daily accountability/management, leadership discipline, and leadership behaviors that were originally developed by David Mann in his book *Creating a Lean Culture: Tools to Sustain Lean Conversions, Second Edition* (Mann 2010).

Leader Standard Work

Leader standard work is an operational performance management tool. It is a list of activities, how they are performed, and the time it takes to complete each of them. All employees in an organization from front-line employees to city managers to deputy ministers can develop leader standard work to streamline their processes and allow them more time for value-added activity.

Leader standard work defines the most efficient way of undertaking normal business processes. It ensures accountability by prioritizing and systemizing work activities to ensure necessary work gets done. Accountability is reinforced when managers and supervisors review employee leader standard work and, if appropriate, put in place any countermeasures in the event work is not completed as planned. Leader standard work helps leaders shift their behavior and it provides continuity of operations when people are away because work processes are clearly defined. Other staff can more easily step in and pick up the work when, for example, employees are on vacation or leave. When developing leader standard work, consider the following questions.

> **What Does Your Workday Look Like?**
>
> - How do you spend your time?
> - What are your main activities?
> - How much time do you spend on coaching and mentoring?
> - How much time are you able to allocate to organizational priorities?
> - What are the opportunities to make changes and free up time?

Encouraging employees to use leader standard work in their day-to-day routine helps them focus on process and behavior, not just results. However, in our experience, putting in place standard work is the most difficult part of Lean Management at all organizations. Management report that employees are reluctant to acknowledge their work is not "special" and their duties can be standardized. While it is true that senior executives may only be able to standardize 10 percent of their work, it is possible for frontline employees to standardize 90 percent of their duties.

When you're able to show someone how their work is contributing to the bigger picture, they become more engaged and productive for the client, for the ministry, and for themselves.

_ Director, Ministry of Economy

Organizations also indicate employees are quick to abandon the discipline of standard work when there is an unexpected workplace issue or crisis. Having said this, once embedded in the organization, leader standard work is invaluable for achieving efficiency and continuous improvement, transitioning employees to new roles and building Lean culture.

Visual Controls

Visual controls in the workplace remind people of standard procedures, reinforce safety, provide feedback, and hold people accountable. They make it easy to measure and compare expected performance with actual results. Lean managers use visual displays or Lean Walls to connect with employees, supervisors, and managers on the floor about how they are feeling about their work, where there are difficulties, and any obstacles to improvement. Visual controls are not about creating "nice" displays of charts and graphs. They can be "quick and dirty" real-time leading measures used to assess and monitor performance, identify improvement opportunities, make adjustments as necessary, and recommit to action. Visual controls encourage everyone to have a disciplined focus and adhere to the Lean processes.

There are all kinds of displays organizations can use in the workplace. People can create SEQDF boards to focus on Safety, Engagement, Quality, Delivery, and Financial Management. Innovation boards can be developed to encourage employees to seek opportunities for innovation in the workplace, share their ideas, and work together to implement them. Team workflow boards can help teams keep better track of employees' workload and progress. Employees can create their own individual workflow boards to help stay organized by writing tasks on a sticky note and categorizing it as "new work," "due today," "to do," "complete," and "past due." Culture Boards can be built to enhance and recognize the organization and team culture.

Daily Accountability/Management

Daily accountability refers to processes that managers undertake with their staff to reinforce and followup on leader standard work and visual controls. The purpose is to identify, focus, and implement opportunities for improvement. Daily management engages staff, ensures follow-up on assignments, promotes project management, and supports problem solving so issues can be resolved quickly. Typical questions would include the following:

> Setting and working towards our goals is nothing new, but when you take that work and put it in a visual format, each employee can actually see the link between his or her work and the bigger picture, and it becomes very empowering. When you continuously see your progress, it's a great reminder of how far you've come, and a big motivation going forward.
> _Manager, Organizational Renewal

> **Do You Practice Lean Management?**
>
> - Do you engage in regular activities to plan and control your business processes?
> - Can you tell if standards are being adhered to and are sufficient?
> - Do you focus on the process?
> - Do you have visual controls in place?
> - Do you measure the amount of time it takes for tasks to be completed?
>
> *This is what leads to continuous improvement*

Structured daily meetings or "huddles" at the start of each day are used by Lean managers to review the previous day's work and planned tasks for the day forward. They are brief, ten- to fifteen minute-long informal stand-up meetings held in the work area. Huddles provide an opportunity to reward employees, ensure focus, and resolve unexpected events which, if not addressed, could impact service delivery.

> When we were deciding how to incorporate the Lean tools into our work, what grabbed us the most was that Lean opened a space for everyone's ideas and input, and had the potential to engage everyone in the process. And we knew it would be important for our team to embrace the process together, rather than have it imposed from the top down.
> _Acting Executive Director

Leadership Discipline

Lean managers need disciplined leadership to make sure the right things get done, at the right time, in the right sequence, as efficiently as possible. They need to ensure leader standard work is followed and updated, as required. They need to engage employees, go on the *Gemba* regularly, make sure visual controls are maintained, ensure daily huddles are occurring across the organization, and regularly assess process and progress. Lean managers need to ensure rigor in the identification of problems and root causes. They need to "plan," "do," "check," and "adjust" as required. They also must ensure people are held accountable, momentum is sustained, and outcomes achieved. This is challenging work which, from our perspective, is made much easier by adoption of a structured Lean Management System within the organization.

> **Lean Managers "Go and See" on the *Gemba***
>
> When on the *Gemba*, ask yourself:
> - What is the purpose of this *Gemba* and of the organization? Are they aligned? Can you see that alignment in the process and the people? Is there "line of sight"?
> - Are processes designed to achieve the purpose?
> - Are people engaged and supported?
> - Ask What? Why? What if? Why not?
> - Identify and act: what can you do to assist, support, and remove barriers

Problem Solving

Training and coaching employees in problem-solving techniques such as root cause analysis, Plan-Do-Check-Adjust (PDCA), and the use of A3s to generate higher performance is a fundamental responsibility of Lean managers. Establishing a standard approach for identifying and dealing with the root causes of problems and issues allows an organization to create a "problem-solving mind-set" which is rooted in fact-based analysis. Training in basic data analysis tools and techniques allows staff to engage in structured problem solving when faced with addressing daily operational issues. As a best practice, areas for improvement are identified and discussed during team huddles, and action plans are identified and agreed upon to complete root cause analysis. Staffers analyze performance issues and use it as an opportunity to continuously improve. As a result, problem solving becomes a way of doing business and is the standard approach used to deal with daily issues and problems.

Leadership Behaviors

Most public-sector organizations have in place a set of organizational values that inspire and outline employee expectations. Many also have clear leadership "competencies" which guide executive recruitment and are the standard to which leaders are held. As organizations progress in their Lean journey, they sometimes find it necessary to revisit their values and competencies to ensure they can be anchored in leadership behaviors.

Leading with Lean requires managers to change the way they interact with employees. While traditional leadership generally involves a hierarchical exercise of power, Lean requires servant leadership[3] where the focus is on mentoring, coaching, and training to empower employees to identify, implement, and sustain improvement. Leadership is exercised through trusting and respecting that employees want to do the best they can for their clients. It requires leaders to interact on a regular basis with frontline employees to ensure they understand organizational priorities and the important role employees play in helping to achieve them. Lean leaders encourage employees to problem-solve and help remove obstacles that may be impeding better, safer service to the customer. They encourage innovation, allow new approaches to be tested, and provide recognition for improvement.

Traditional Leadership	Lean Leadership
• Hierarchical • Top-down • Siloed • People are independent • Managers firefight • Risk adverse • Failure is punished	• Leaders as mentors, coaches, and trainers • Focused on results, alignment, process, and people

Lean leadership also requires executives to be comfortable interacting directly with clients to get their perspectives on how programs and services can better meet their needs and expectations. Leading with humility and respect is a Lean mantra and Lean organizations require executives who follow this mantra.

There are three broad areas of leadership and management competencies that intersect in strong public sector Lean organizations: people, continuous improvement, and system competencies. Strong leaders build relationships, motivate others, bring teams together, are not afraid to address conflict, and manage performance. They also lead change within the organization and across systems, foster innovation, and continuously strive

---

[3] The term "servant leadership" was coined in 1970 by Robert K. Greenleaf in an essay The Servant as Leader.

to improve outcomes. In addition, they demonstrate critical thinking, engage in system thinking, manage change, and influence and set policy.

As an organization progresses in its Lean journey, senior leaders and managers need to adjust their leadership style in accordance with Lean Management. This may require coaching support since it can be challenging for anyone, including leaders and managers, to learn new behaviors. A variety of resources are available such as improvement plan templates, guides to leadership walks and visibility walls, problem-solving methods and so on. The key to getting results is commitment, discipline, and a willingness to learn and adapt.

Unfortunately, in our experience, not all leaders will successfully make the transition and public sector Lean organizations, like private sector ones, must be prepared to deal with these human resource issues. While some leaders and managers will voluntarily move on, some may need to be given a helping hand. As a senior executive recently told us, *"Lean leadership is corporate direction. We expect everyone to get on board and recognize that, for some, it will be more challenging than for others. However, bottom line? Opting out is not an option."*

Lean Management System

While much has been written describing *what* Lean leadership and management is, little information is available describing *how* to implement it within public-sector organizations. We believe augmenting the existing management style with a structured approach is ideal for ensuring that Lean improvement is aligned with organizational strategy, and the initiative is cascaded throughout the organization and sustained in the long term. We refer to this as implementation of a Lean Management System and it can help enable a Lean culture to grow and flourish within public sector organizations.

A Lean Management System equips frontline supervisors, managers, and executive managers with the skills and tools to manage effectively in a Lean organization and foster a culture of continuous improvement. In a very deliberate, disciplined way it operationalizes the principal elements of Lean Management so that work is aligned, performance is visual, there is clear accountability for processes and value streams, huddles and other processes are established for communicating openly and frequently with staff, problem-solving capacity is increased, measurement and reporting systems are put in place and regularly reviewed, cultural change is fostered, mentoring and coaching occurs, performance is recognized, and success is celebrated. Simply put, it is about instilling behavioral change in the organization to lever improvement.

Organizations adopt a "See, Do, and Lead" approach to developing internal Lean Leaders and implementing a Lean Management System across the organization. Lean Leaders in training observe an experienced Lean Leader lead a work area through implementation of key elements of a Lean Management System. The Lean Leaders in training then lead implementation in another work area with support from the experienced Lean Leader. After this, Lean Leaders are ready to independently lead and implement Lean Management in other work areas within work units and across the organization.

As the following case studies show, embedding a Lean Management System to transform the behaviors of the management team and, in turn, those of frontline employees is a real challenge. Behavioral change does not come easily and requires training, practice, and continuous feedback to optimize what managers do, how they do it, and the tools they use. Managers need to change the way they spend their time to coach and problem-solve with staff. This requires discipline and rigor, and may need to be undertaken branch by branch, over time, to ensure behavioral change is sustained.

CASE STUDY
Insurance Corporation of British Columbia (ICBC), Canada

The Insurance Corporation of British Columbia (ICBC), a provincial Crown corporation, has approximately 4,800 employees. One of BC's largest corporations and among Canada's largest property and casualty (P&C) insurers, it oversees a vast enterprise that includes issuing drivers licenses, vehicle registration, and road safety. Its insurance products and services are available through a province-wide network of approximately 900 independent brokers, government agents, and appointed agents. ICBC processes approximately 900,000 claims annually through its 24/7 telephone claims handling facility, thirty-eight claim centers, and other claims handling facilities across the province. ICBC also provides driver licensing services through 120 points of service, including driver licensing centers and government agents. All BC motorists do business with the ICBC.

The Corporation launched its Operational Excellence program, based on Lean thinking management principles, in 2013. Today it is an enterprise-wide program that touches all business areas within ICBC. Operational Excellence is a core element of ICBC's business strategy, with a goal to create a customer-centric organization and a culture of continuous improvement.

ICBC implemented Lean management principles in two major customer-facing business operations: Claims Customer Service and Driver Licensing Offices. Lean Management principles designed specifically to drive changes in staff mind-sets and behaviors were introduced in a structured manner to improve service and create an environment of problem solving and ongoing improvement.

The Challenge

Claims Customer Service's Dial-a-Claim contact center works with customers on more than nine hundred thousand claims annually. Claim volume continues to grow since there are more vehicles on the road, more crashes and other factors.

Prior to the rollout of Operational Excellence in this business area, a new claim system had just been implemented and the new operational data reporting was gradually coming online. With the new system, new processes, and new operating approach, there was a need to holistically revisit operational performance to determine fresh standards. Leadership had to start again to determine if the business area was operating at an acceptable level of performance or whether there was opportunity for further improvement.

The Approach

As part of the rollout of Operational Excellence, four key elements of Lean Management principles were introduced:

1. Information centers: Information Centers (IC) were established to make team performance visible by way of whiteboards or the use of OneNote for teams managed remotely. For adjusters, four key performance indicators (KPIs) that aligned to the team and to the overall vision, purpose, and goals of the organization were established and tracked on the IC. ICs were aligned vertically from the unit level up to the full Claims Customer Service level. Adjusters, unit managers, operations managers, and the director began receiving weekly reporting on performance against these four indicators with information presented so that everyone could see their performance trends regardless of their level of responsibility.
2. Huddles and performance reviews: Weekly team huddles were established to assess performance, drive accountability, and improve teamwork. Huddles occur on Tuesdays to review the previous week's operational results. Unit huddles occur in the early morning and are followed by area huddles in the late morning. The Claims Customer Service huddle occurs at 2 p.m. so that issues and problems are escalated up to the Senior Director level within hours of being raised by the frontline staff. For example, the 2015 leap year was the first one in which the new claims system was in effect. On March 1, at the morning huddle, staff identifed an issue related to coverage on February 29 for customers whose policy normally expired on February 28. By 4 p.m. the same day, guidance was provided to 2,500 staff on how to handle claims made on February 29 to ensure continued consistent quality service to their customers.
3. Routines and practices: Practices were embedded in the daily routines of supervisors and managers to reinforce coaching and improve workforce skills. This helped to drive a culture of change and improvement. One approach taken to identify coaching opportunities was to have the staff complete a skills matrix about all job duties within the department. The managers and supervisors also rated staff. Where gaps were identified, the supervisors then scheduled coaching and/or training sessions with the staff based on the standards set in the department. This is an ongoing process and as a result, staff have become much more confident in handling their work, reduced the time to complete their activities and the number of questions has also been reduced. Scheduling has become streamlined as the staff grows more proficient in all activities. This has also cut scheduling time for the supervisors.
4. Problem solving: Employees were coached on problem-solving techniques (Data analysis, 5-whys, Fishbone, Value Stream Mapping, 5S) and escalation routes to assist higher performance. The Dial-a-Claim department held numerous problem-solving events following the training, including completing the 5-whys when the area was struggling

to meet a year-end target for Average Handle Time per call. With this tool, the team quickly identified issues, put plans in place, and the target was met. More recently the department initiated a Value Stream Mapping (VSM) event regarding car seat reimbursements. In a huddle, a staff member raised this as a problem area, and this issue was documented on the Information Center. The reimbursements process was cumbersome, outdated and lacked transparency for customers. A team was put together for a VSM and as a result corporate policy changes are being made to provide an updated, streamlined, and customer-friendly approach. These changes will reduce the processing time for staff by 50 percent, and more importantly, provide a much more timely and simple process for customers.

Over a period of eight weeks, in addition to making several changes to claims allocation (based on claim complexity and adjuster expertise), Dial-a-Claim was immersed in cycles of learning and Plan, Do, Check, Act (PDCA) through repeated processes of training, designing, implementing, and reviewing each of the four elements. The detailed, structured discussions with the team focused on customer value and led to a clear definition and agreement on what the team needed to do each day. Once this was agreed on, daily coaching was established with leadership shadowing employees in order to observe how they were doing against set KPIs and to help them to achieve these consistently.

Frontline managers and staff embraced this new way of working as they started to see value in incorporating these elements in their daily work. Clarity of purpose has also changed behavior towards problem solving and customer service. People are eager to come forward with their problem-solving ideas rather than immediately looking to managers for answers. Positive customer feedback that the team regularly receives is displayed on the IC. This has reinforced the need for teamwork and improved staff morale.

Some of the most notable changes in the business area include:

- Jumping to solutions has been replaced with fact-based and structured root cause analysis and thoughtful solution identification, validation, and implementation resulting in more sustainable improvements.
- Staff and frontline managers are empowered to call out problems, and the problems are being fixed.
- Managers, including new managers, spend more time engaging with frontline staff in problem solving and coaching.
- Staff are realizing the potential of Lean and Lean Management principles to further improve how they work, remove barriers and non-value-added work, and create new capacity to improve customer service.

The Results

The most significant result the business area has realized is the change in staff mind-sets and behaviors. A culture of constructive feedback, a greater understanding of the business from an end-to-end process perspective, and a more engaged team has developed.

Quantitative benefits realized within two months of the rollout of Operational Excellence in this business area include:

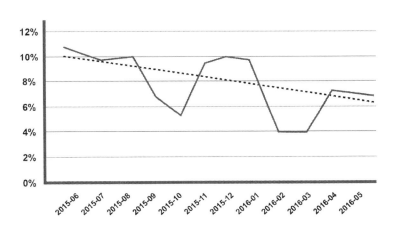

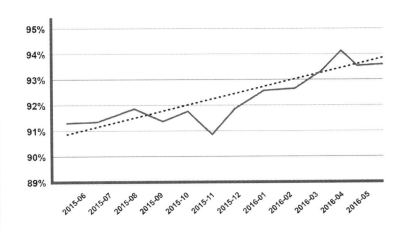

- Call abandonment rate dropping from 10.6 percent to 6.3 percent from June 2015 to May 2016
- A 15.7 percent increase in call volume was absorbed with a 5.6 percent increase in staffing levels
- Contact center staff schedule adherence went up from 91 percent to 94 percent_ representing a savings of 4 FTE.
- 50 percent improvement in adjuster productivity; monthly claims closed per adjuster improved from 57.8 per FTE to 83.6 FTE from Q1 2015 to Q1 2016.

Looking at what has been achieved at Claim Customer Service through Operational Excellence, implemented over a short period of two to three months, it must be noted that *none* of the changes were fueled by technology. Investing in people and introducing new ways to approach and complete work is the way to sustain improvements and get the most from business operations.

CASE STUDY
Lower Mainland Facilities Management (LMFM), British Columbia, Canada

Lower Mainland Facilities Management (LMFM) provides services to Fraser Health, Providence Health Care, the Provincial Health Services Authority, and Vancouver Coastal Health in the Province of British Columbia. LMFM is one of the largest full-service facilities management organizations in Canada and it chose Vancouver General Hospital as the pilot site for implementing PwC's Perform Lean Management System. The focus was on identifying areas of waste within the work order management process to release capacity and address the work order backlog. The backlog impacted customer service, patient care, and the life span of capital assets such as elevators, HVAC systems, and so on. Working closely, the site leadership and fifty-five employees from eight maintenance shops (Carpentry, Locks, Paint, Plumbing, HVAC, Electrical, Machine, and General Maintenance) improved ways of working and empowered employees to make changes.

The Challenge

Vancouver General Hospital was facing an increasing work order backlog which impacted customer service expectations of the clinical partners, patient care, and the stewardship of the physical assets. The demand and preventative maintenance requirements exceeded the staff's capacity to deliver. The compliance rate for critical assets was also identified as a priority by the Risk Management program. Additionally, LMFM hoped to prove the concept of Lean in order to acquire operating budget funding for the initiation of an Integrated Workspace Management System.

The Approach

Over a period of twelve weeks, LMFM implemented the ten elements of the Perform Lean Management System. They built capacity by training eight team leads who, in turn, trained employees and systematically implemented ideas from a Value Stream Mapping event.

The maintenance manager and site manager proactively increased leadership visibility at the shops, improved two-way communication, and provided employees with an opportunity to engage in problem-solving sessions. They also increased accountability by setting targets for each shop and making progress visible on information centers by using daily progress reviews. They engaged staff at all levels and improved the interaction between shops. This empowered employees to proactively identify and solve problems, and take on a continuous improvement mind-set.

> **The Results**
>
> During the twelve-week phase of work, the following benefits were realized:
>
> - 72 percent increase in average daily preventative maintenance (PM) work order completions, resulting in significant improvements in PM compliance for several critical assets
> - 29 percent improvement in average number of work orders completed per week
> - 42 percent reduction in total work order backlog, which includes demand maintenance and preventative maintenance
> - 2 to 3 FTEs capacity gain from reducing motion waste by implementing a zone-based model and increasing Hands-on-Tool time
>
> Post-implementation, the staff achieved 28 percent in additional work order backlog reduction, bringing the total backlog reduction achieved to 58 percent.

Strategic Use of Lean

Organizations embarking on their Lean journey often do so with considerable caution. They may initially see Lean as an experiment and want to test it out, or pilot it, before committing more fully. Also, because they are inexperienced, they may not fully understand Lean or its potential. For this reason, in the early phases of implementation organizations often shy from taking on major value streams, especially citizen-facing programs, services, and processes. These may be seen as too risky and, as a result, internal administrative or peripheral processes may be tackled first.

From our perspective, this is not problematic. When getting started, we believe an organization should just start and gain experience and familiarity with Lean. Once it does so, it will see some early gains and will better understand the potential for using Lean to move forward its core business. However, even when an organization begins tackling larger, more customer-facing processes, it may not be doing so in a strategic way.

Ideally, there should be alignment between the organization's strategic plan and improvement work that is underway in the organization. Unfortunately, this is often not the case and administrative and frontline improvement activity can be disconnected from strategic priority areas.

Value Stream Identification and Selection

It can be helpful for an organization to identify all its key value streams and develop a sequenced plan for Lean improvement that is guided by strategic priorities. Usually this occurs when the organization begins to incorporate Lean as part of its organizational transformation effort – when it is moving from initiating Lean to integrating it into the way it does business. Lean organizations have multi-year improvement plans for internal and customer-facing programs, services, and processes. These plans include the direct engagement of clients in improvement events to ensure customer service is at the forefront of service delivery.

One approach is for the executive team to identify the organization's key competencies and the major functions, programs, services, activities, processes, and systems within each of those competencies. They can then categorize each as core (inherent to the delivery of the service), enabling (supports the delivery of the service), or ad hoc (an occasional activity that impacts core or enabling activity). This can help the executive team to then assess the performance of each function from the perspective of the customer and, as well, based on effectiveness and efficiency. They will then be well positioned to identify and prioritize major value streams for improvement as well as develop a multiyear Lean improvement plan.

Figure 5-2
Strategic Value Stream Selection Process

Using Lean Thinking to Address Complex Issues

It is also possible to use Lean concepts, approaches, or "Lean thinking" to help address major, complex issues facing an organization. Problem identification and root cause analysis can assist organizations to bring more focus to their strategies and interventions. Seeing issues through the eyes of the customer or client, and "value" from the perspective of the citizen, can lead to innovative solutions. The discipline involved can add rigor to evidence gathering, measurement, the identification of targets, and monitoring and reporting systems. Because of its value stream perspective,

Lean can help break down organizational silos, lead to experimentation, and unify people to "row in the same direction, together."

As Figure 5-3 shows, organizations that use Lean strategically have alignment from the top-down and the bottom-up. Employees understand the organization's strategic priorities and their role in contributing through improvement. Similarly, by engaging directly with their employees, executive leadership has a greater appreciation for tactical challenges. Across the organization, people are aligned and working together to achieve common goals.

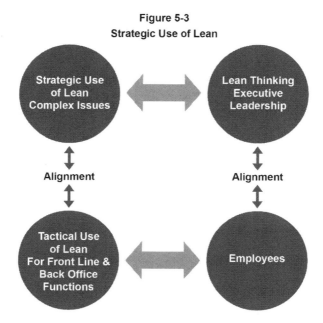

CASE STUDY
Results Washington

In September 2013, Governor Jay Inslee issued Executive Order 13-04, which stated, in part, that:

> *Washington state and its public servants are committed to the continuous improvement of services, outcomes and performance of state government, to realize a safe, beautiful and healthy place to live and work. In order to achieve these aims, "Results Washington," an innovative, data-driven, performance management initiative will drive the operations of state government through Lean thinking. This initiative will aid state leaders in fact-based decision-making, enhancing the breadth of understanding, focus and commitment to our customers — all Washingtonians.*

Results Washington brings together two previously run independent initiatives: the Government Management and Accountability Program (GMAP) and Lean. Prior to the Executive Order, Lean was implemented in some state departments and agencies on an ad hoc tactical basis with the assistance of private sector partners such as Boeing. Results Washington is now taking Lean management to a new level because it is using Lean principles at both a strategic and tactical level to deliver on the governor's priorities.

The Challenge

Prior to initiation of Results Washington, actionable goals were established by the state administration which had a long history of process improvement and quality management. While early Lean efforts in some departments and agencies had shown success, agencies were working in silos with very little cross-agency collaboration. The state's performance management efforts at the time were viewed as too rigid and compliance-oriented rather than focusing on collaboration, root cause analysis, and the voice of the customer.

The new governor, Jay Inslee, elected in late 2012, was committed to improving the state of the economy, access to healthcare and education, and addressing some of the deep-rooted social issues facing Washingtonians. He was also committed to eliminating waste in government. A decision was made to broaden the application of Lean to create a culture of continuous improvement across all state agencies as a means of delivering on government's priorities.

The Approach

Lean thinking was applied strategically in the assessment and development of solutions to address key challenges. A framework was developed for citizen and employee engagement, cross-agency collaboration, reporting, and sharing of results with the public. It articulated five key goal areas for Results Washington:

1. World-class education: Preparing every Washingtonian for a healthy and productive life, including success in a job or career in the community and as a lifelong learner
2. Prosperous economy: Fostering an innovative economy where businesses, workers, and communities thrive in every corner of the state
3. Sustainable energy and a clean environment: Building a legacy of resource stewardship for the next generation of Washingtonians
4. Healthy and safe communities: fostering the health of Washingtonians from a healthy start to a safe and supported future
5. Efficient, effective, and accountable government: fostering a Lean culture that drives accountability and results for the people of Washington

Within each of the five goal areas, measures, targets, and timelines were established with input from hundreds of Washingtonians, dozens of stakeholder groups, and state agencies.

Specific goal maps were established for each of the five goal areas. For example, the healthy and safe communities goal includes efforts such as:

- Decreasing the infant mortality rate from 5.1 per 1,000 births in 2012 to 4.4 or fewer per 1,000 births by 2016
- Increasing toddler vaccination rates from 65.2 percent in 2012 to 72.6 percent by 2016
- Decreasing violent infractions prison rates from 1.0 to .9 per 100 offenders by 2017.

In total, there are 192 measures, with an agency director assigned to each as lead.

Each goal also has a Goal Council made up of agency directors which meets monthly to review progress, share data, refine strategies, and collaborate on action items. These meetings often include partner organizations outside state government. Cross-agency collaboration is important. The lead for reducing homelessness, for example, is the Department of Commerce, which works collaboratively with the departments related to health, veterans, education, and social services, as well as local nonprofit groups, counties, and cities.

Ten times each year (twice per Goal Council), the governor meets with individual goal councils to discuss what has been working effectively or not and how to improve results. Customers and clients such as ex-offenders, homeless people, students, farmers, tree growers, adults with intellectual disabilities, veterans, and so on are often invited. These meetings are televised and archived online to reinforce messages of transparency, accountability, and citizen involvement. A liaison to the State Auditor, a separately elected official in Washington state, is also assigned full-time to the program, and one-on-one meetings are conducted with many of the 147 state legislators.

The entire initiative is overseen by the governor and his top executive team, notably the Chief of Staff and Deputy Chief of Staff. The Director of the Results Washington office works closely with a "Design Team" made up of the five Goal Council leads, and Results Washington staff work closely with the following partners:

- Accountability Partners (Policy & Budget, Deputy Directors, Human Resources staff), and Department of Enterprise Services (Lean Training & Workforce Development)
- Strategic Partners (Private Sector Partners, Legislators, Auditor's Office, Lean agency Advisors, Communication Directors, and Data/Performance Management directors)
- Engagement Partners (53+ Agencies, Boards and Commissions, and Stakeholders)

A variety of Lean training has been developed and is available to employees at all levels including Lean knowledge and skills training, leaders-as-coaches training for middle managers, problem-solving workshops, and Lean improvement (Plan, Do, Check, Adjust) workshops. Support is also available to assist in the development of enterprise/program maps. There is also a Lean Advisory Group with agency representation that meets monthly to discuss issues and opportunities. The State has also developed a Lean Fellowship Program to build capacity in State departments and agencies. More than twenty-eight thousand employees have had Lean knowledge and skills training, including thousands of managers and supervisors. Also, more than 750 employees are now trained facilitators. From 2013 to 2015, almost four thousand employees directly participated in Lean improvements and, from 2013 through 2015, state employees took part in more than two thousand improvement projects.

When asked how they have managed to engage so many people within and outside government, officials report they are united by the clarity of the goals and their commitment to the targets that they have been part of establishing. They also see the value in working together in a new way; for example, the Healthy Weight Youth initiative is working closely with Education, Transportation, Health, and the farming community to provide healthy eating options for youth.

Results Washington stands out because departments are united enterprise-wide in collaborating to achieve a very clear set of strategic priorities established by the governor. While the group acknowledges it still has a long way to go before Lean is fully a part of the organization's DNA, the participants believe they are making significant progress in addressing long-standing, complex issues and problems. Key has been the Lean methodology which has brought a citizen perspective to everything they do and has helped bring focus and discipline to strategies, interventions, measurement, monitoring, and reporting.

The Results
In Education

- More families of high-risk young children are able to receive voluntary home visits from trained professionals who provide support and information about maternal and child health, parenting, and child development.
- Fewer college students need remedial courses. The rate dropped from 40 percent in the 2009_2010 school year to 33.2 percent in the 2013_2014 school year.
- More college students are enrolling in employer high-demand programs. More than five thousand additional students enrolled in such programs from the 2010_2011 to the 2014_2015 school years.
- The number of college students taking online courses rose by more than four thousand in two years.
- A record number of students _ 91 percent of those who are eligible _ signed up for the College Bound Scholarship Program in the 2014_2015 school year.
- The four-year graduation rate for high school students rose from 76 percent (class of 2013) to 77.2 percent (class of 2014) to 78.1 percent (class of 2015).

The Economy

- From 2011 to 2014, exports increased 42 percent, small business income increased 16 percent, and average worker earnings increased 10 percent.
- Employment in key sectors has also risen. From 2011 through 2014, employment rose 31 percent in information/communication technology, 54 percent in maritime, and 11 percent in agriculture.
- From 2012 to 2014, Washington's ranking for innovation and entrepreneurship rose from 13th in the country to third.

The Environment

- The percentage of Endangered Species Act-listed salmon and

steelhead populations at healthy, sustainable levels increased from 16 percent in 2010 to 21 percent in 2015.
- The percentage of Washingtonians living in a place where air quality meets federal standards rose from 92 percent in 2014 to 100 percent in 2015.
- Diesel soot in the air is half of what it was a decade ago and more than three thousand old woodstoves have been replaced with cleaner alternatives in the past five years.
- Outdoor recreation rates are rising in Washington's public lands and waters.
- The percentage of endangered, threatened, or sensitive wildlife species considered to be recovering has risen from 28 percent in 2013 to 30 percent in 2015.

In Health & Safety

- Cigarette smoking by 10th graders continues to decline, from 13 percent in 2011 to 8 percent in 2014.
- Teen drinking is also decreasing with the percentage of 10th graders reporting drinking alcohol in the past month dropping from 28 percent in 2010 to 21 percent in 2014.
- Compared to two years ago, nearly fifteen thousand more adults received state outpatient mental health services.
- Recidivism is down among youth released from juvenile rehabilitation facilities. In 2012, 8 percent of youth returned to rehabilitation within a year. In 2014, that number dropped to 5 percent.
- The number of ex-offenders getting jobs after release from prison increased from 31 percent in 2013 to 38.1 percent at the end of 2015.
- Speed-related traffic deaths dropped from 184 in 2013 to 156 in 2015.
- Washington has the second-lowest worker fatality rate in the nation.
- The teen pregnancy rate is half of what it was in 2008. Among fifteen- to seventeen-year-olds, the pregnancy rate in 2008 was nearly twenty-seven out of one thousand girls. In 2014, the rate was 13.3.

In Government

- Employee-driven Lean improvements at the tactical level in dozens of agencies have resulted in easier-to-understand forms, streamlined processes, faster services, better outcomes, cost avoidance, more transparency, and higher customer satisfaction.

Lean Maturity Assessment

Following several years of experience with Lean, executive leadership may choose to assess their public-sector organization's maturity with respect to Lean implementation. A variety of assessment tools are available to assist in this process; some are more sophisticated than others. The purpose is to determine how embedded Lean is within the culture of the organization, identify strengths and weaknesses, and develop plans for improvement. Self-assessment approaches can be utilized; however, ideally, maturity assessments should be conducted by an external party to ensure they are unbiased and objective. The following case study describes Export Development Canada's (EDC) transformational program and the role an external maturity assessment conducted by the Shingo Institute played in helping EDC take the next steps in its Lean journey.

CASE STUDY
Export Development Canada (EDC)

Export Development Canada (EDC) is Canada's export credit agency, an enterprise wholly owned by the Government of Canada. Its mandate is to support and develop trade between Canada and other countries, and sustain Canada's competitiveness in the international marketplace. EDC provides financing and insurance solutions in support of Canadian trade and uses knowledge and relationships to connect Canadian capabilities to international opportunities.

EDC was founded in 1944. Its corporate headquarters is located in Ottawa and it has seventeen regional offices across Canada, and permanent representations in twelve foreign markets. EDC has seven thousand customers in 198 countries, contributes to 4 percent of Canada's GDP, and supports 568,799 jobs. It has approximately 1,350 full-time employees. EDC competes in the open market, is self-sustaining and pays dividends to its shareholder, the Government of Canada.

The Challenge

The period 1997_2007 was particularly challenging for EDC. Annual growth in Canadian exports of goods and services was one of the lowest of OECD countries and, indeed, lower than the world average. EDC was experiencing a significant drop in revenue. EDC's forty billion-dollar portfolio was riddled with long cycle times and relatively complex transactions. Customers of EDC's financing business were dissatisfied and employee morale was at an all-time low.

The Approach

A transformation program based on Lean thinking was conceived to focus on customer value and drive change in staff mind-sets and behaviors. The CEO launched the "EDC Way," a transformative program to drive efficiency improvements and metrics-focused behavior, initially in the financing business. Lean experts were engaged to assist with end-to-end process reviews. The organization faced significant resistance at the beginning, with staff making comments such as: "...this is not manufacturing _ we are different _ this won't work here...you can't standardize what I do...I'm an artist...you want to turn me into a monkey with a keyboard...." The organization persevered, focusing on simplifying core processes within the financing business as well as in the bonding and credit insurance business. Employee engagement was extended to include both frontline sales staff as well as back office operations staff. Customers were engaged to better understand their pain points.

The various improvement events in the businesses delivered significant initial results in terms of efficiency improvements and capacity creation. However, performance started to slip over time. Complexity began to creep back into core processes. The organization started to assess its maturity in Lean transformation and question the sustainability of results of the transformation itself. Three key areas emerged in the assessment of the organization's Lean maturity: (1) the recognition that more work needs to be done in changing the culture of the organization through a focused effort to bring mind-set and behavior change to all levels of the organization; (2) adoption of the Shingo model for Operational Excellence as a framework and yardstick for the EDC Way; and (3) further drive executive engagement. Following the assessment, EDC committed to reinvigorate its transformation program by focusing on the following:

- Improve executive communication
- Establish standard work for leaders
- Refocus on continuous improvement, not just big projects
- Figure out the EDC Way of working

The development of the EDC Way of working involved assessing various quality and continuous improvement models and management systems and "connecting the dots" to what is working and what is not working at EDC. The following framework for the EDC Way was developed, communicated, and implemented throughout the organization:

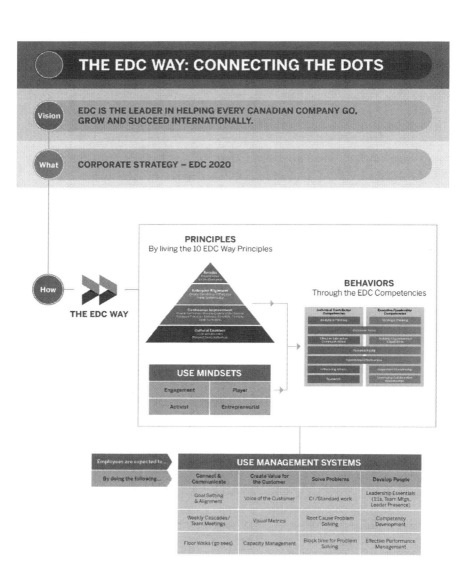

DELIVERING RESULTS THAT MATTER

THE EDC WAY: CONNECTING THE DOTS

"WHY?" TALKING POINTS

	Connect & Communicate	Create Value for the Customer	Solve Problems	Develop People
We are expected to do this because...	Connecting and communicating through all levels of the organization creates constancy of purpose and links every individual to the overall objectives of EDC. This creates an environment where everyone knows that they are working on the right things and creating value for the customer.	Once we know that we are working on the right things we need to know how we are doing "are we winning or losing?" as we work to create value for the customer. And when we are "losing" we know it so we can problem solve.	The point of improvement is to make things better, faster, easier and cheaper for our customers. We do this in two ways: 1) By problem solving to improve the process and 2) By developing our people	As we train and coach to develop our people we become more capable and effective at creating value for the customer.
We will look for...	• Transparent sharing of information • Constancy of purpose • A focus on the long term	• Measuring what matters • Behaviours aligned with performance • Identifying cause and effect relationships	• Standard and stable processes • Identification and elimination of waste • Simple and visual	• A safe environment • Everyone is involved and empowered • Identified opportunities for development
Why do we need to do this now?	We need to up our game because: • We need to be more relevant to existing and potential customers • The external environment is changing faster than ever before • Our customers' expectations are higher and rising • We need to be better at solving the right problems (which affect our customers) • And we need to do all of this in a financially sustainable manner			

The framework provides a reference point, with expectations of leadership and norms in the organization. In order to embed the EDC Way principles and behaviors in the psyche of the organization, EDC invested heavily in technical and behavioral coaching for the leadership and ongoing enterprise-wide assessment of the transformation program. The EDC Way is based on the premise that leaders must spend time in the workplace on a regular basis, engage, and coach employees in identifying root causes of problems, implement standard work, and measure and monitor performance. The organization completed two enterprise-wide assessments spaced one year apart. One hundred percent of the organization was assessed over three weeks by nine individuals. One-hundred thirty-five leaders and three-hundred and eighty-seven frontline staff, representing 39 percent of the total organization, were interviewed. Each of the nine senior vice presidents received a scorecard against the four EDC Way Management System pillars and a development plan was prepared with each executive.

The Results

Changes in the organization's culture and leadership behavior have been the primary benefits of EDC's transformation program. "Humility and respect," a key Lean trait required in leadership, is clearly visible and demonstrated on a daily basis. Individual coaches assigned to senior executives provide ongoing feedback on style and behavior, with the objective to promote ideal behavior and live the EDC Way in the best possible fashion.

Chapter 6

LEAN STRATEGIC PLANNING AND DEPLOYMENT

To ensure they deliver results, some Lean organizations use a structured approach to the planning and deployment cycle. They determine goals, develop plans to achieve those goals, create measures which are monitored to track progress, and make course corrections along the way. Often referred to as *Hoshin Kanri*, a Japanese phrase that means management of the strategic direction-setting process, this approach is an efficient way to link an organization's strategic plan with a disciplined process to ensure the plan is implemented, adapted, and improved over time.

Many public-sector organizations have clear plans, but struggle to translate those plans into practice. Senior managers may be removed from the frontline and consequently, don't understand that the "the devil is in the details." In fact, Lean strategic planning and deployment can help unite an organization around a single plan, engage employees in the common purpose of implementing the plan, and hold participants accountable. It can help an organization sustain Lean and achieve breakthroughs in processes, programs, and services.

Lean strategic planning and deployment turns the planning and deployment process on its head. Traditional organizations spend a great deal of time on planning, and less on deployment. With *Hoshin Kanri*, while the plan is important, deployment is the focus, along with the ability to make adjustments as required. This execution tool helps position a strategic plan throughout the organization by aligning people, activities, and performance metrics with strategic priorities.

The Process

Leaders begin Lean strategic planning and deployment by identifying their "true north": the business needs that must be achieved by the organization and expressed appropriately to make an emotional statement and create a sense of excitement (Dennis, 2009). Paramount is the voice of the customer. The leaders engage staff in an organization-wide review of overall performance. Leaders then create a set of enduring strategies, develop clear outcome statements with timelines, and identify improvement targets (also with timelines). They also articulate what they see as a few vital short-term "must do, can't fail" breakthrough *hoshins*.

This high-level plan is then passed down through the organization in a process sometimes referred to as "catch-ball." The divisions, branches, and units then create their own plan in support of deployment of the high-level plan. This allows the entire organization to become aligned and each unit understands its role in achieving the established goals. Employees see how the work they do contributes to the overall plan. This entire discussion is critical to creating the engagement culture that underpins Lean transformation.

Facilitators of Lean strategic planning and deployment use a few tools to help articulate the plan and make it visual. A matrix is drafted defining what must be achieved in the next three to five years, as well as the breakthrough *hoshin*s for each fiscal year. Also, detailed project plans called A3s are prepared to define problems, activities, timelines, and resources and establish measures and targets. These are displayed on an organization's information center or "visibility wall" which is updated and "walked" on a regular basis by leaders who use the wall to track progress and reinforce accountability. As plans are cascaded down within the organization, each division, branch, and unit develops its own visibility wall. This disciplined structure builds in the "plan," "do," "check," and "adjust" process characterized by Lean Management.

The Visibility Wall

Visibility walls, often known as "viz" walls, are information centers filled with data and measures that enable the organization to monitor the progress made toward achieving desired outcomes articulated in the *Hoshin Kanri* plan. These measures are then reviewed during visibility *wall walks.* The visibility wall and the wall walk are mechanisms for creating insightful discussions, collaborative problem solving, clear actions, and shared responsibility for improvement. Visibility walls are located in central, well-traveled locations within the organization and, increasingly, are posted electronically to make them readily available to leaders, managers, and staff who may be located off-site.

In public-sector organizations, visibility walls may exist at various levels, for example:

- Level 1: Enterprise-wide to include all executives in an organization or across a health or education sector;
- Level 2: Individual departments, ministries, school divisions, or health regions;
- Level 3: Divisions or branches, schools or hospitals; and
- Level 4: Units and/or frontline services, classrooms, wards.

There is no "right" way to prepare a viz wall. The wall should be organized in a manner that makes sense for those who walk the wall. Visibility walls evolve over time as users learn what works best for their organization. Figure 6-1 shows an information center template which provides a starting point for development of a visibility wall.

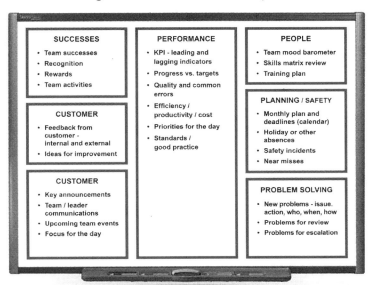

Figure 6-1 Information Center Template

The data used on a visibility wall is intended to inform discussion and decisions related to deployment of the *Hoshin Kanri* strategy. Therefore, the data needs to be the most accurate and up-to-date at that time. Anyone viewing the wall will understand what is going well and is on target and what is off target and needs correction. The data on the wall should help make issues transparent and assist with problem solving that occurs at regularly scheduled wall walks.

Selecting the right measures is challenging work. For improvement purposes, indicators of performance that can be assessed quickly and easily are usually preferable to a more time-consuming and exacting measure. The best data will be relevant to the outcomes and *hoshins* identified in the plan, clear and easy to understand, detailed enough to inform future action, robust enough to allow for trend identification, and accurate. It is important to include targets and have data that is responsive enough to show progress from one wall walk to the next.

When displayed on the wall, measures should be color-coded to indicate status:

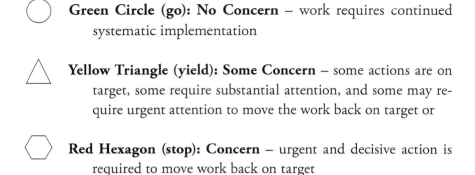

- **Green Circle (go): No Concern** – work requires continued systematic implementation
- **Yellow Triangle (yield): Some Concern** – some actions are on target, some require substantial attention, and some may require urgent attention to move the work back on target or
- **Red Hexagon (stop): Concern** – urgent and decisive action is required to move work back on target

A Corrective Action Plan should be prepared and posted for areas of concern (yellow or red status icons) and updated on a regular basis.

The Wall Walk

Visibility wall walks are brief, focused conversations, held regularly by the wall's "owners" (for example, executives for Level 1, department leadership for Level 2, division or branch staff for Level 3, unit or frontline staff for Level 4) during which the following occurs:

- Progress towards achieving the target is reported by the primary owner as identified in the A3 (project plan);
- Achievements of significant milestones are celebrated;
- Off-target work is identified and plans for course correction are shared. If the plan for course correction is uncertain or if previous attempts at course correction have proved insufficient, focused discussions to understand the root causes of off-target work and to seek solutions are initiated by the primary owner or wall walk participants. Participants are encouraged to ask "Why?" to dig to the root of the issue;
- Potential courses of future action are identified.

The frequency of wall walks increases as the *Hoshin Kanri* plan is cascaded within the organization. Executives, for example, may walk the Level 1 wall three times a year while departments may walk their Level 2 walls monthly. Level 3 walls may be walked even more frequently, possibly weekly, and frontline staff at Level 4 may review the progress of their work daily since their discussions will be focused on everyday improvement and should exemplify the Plan-Do-Check-Adjust (PDCA) cycle.

To maximize the effectiveness of the wall walk, participants should review materials on the wall ahead of time so they are aware of the status of projects and can formulate potential questions for the target's primary owner. Initially, wall walks will likely be longer than desired and a bit stiff. However, as participants gain experience with wall walk report outs, they will become increasingly focused. As a result, wall walks will become shorter and the value of discussion will improve.

Ideally, wall walks should follow an agenda and be facilitated to keep the report outs and related question and answer periods to the point. Items requiring more in-depth discussion may be placed on a debrief parking lot at the suggestion of the facilitator, owners, or participants. Wall walks can then be followed immediately by a debriefing to enable in-depth discussion, if required.

As owners report out at the wall, items identified as status green should just be recognized as being on target. A protracted report out is neither necessary nor appropriate. The exception will be when a significant milestone has been accomplished and time is taken to celebrate. Items identified as yellow or red will require more time on the agenda to enable problem solving and the identification of solutions. These items should also have corrective action plans in place and posted on the wall. These plans should identify work that needs to be completed prior to the next wall walk in an effort to get the work back on target.

Visibility walls and use of wall walks are key Lean tools used as part of the *Hoshin Kanri* planning and deployment process. They help unite the organization in the common purpose of deploying the plan, and they hold participants accountable.

CASE STUDY
Using Lean Strategic Planning and Deployment (*Hoshin Kanri*) Across Saskatchewan's Healthcare System

In the heart of the Canadian prairies, the province of Saskatchewan is home to more than 1.15 million residents (2016 estimate).[4] Healthcare services are directly administered by twelve regional health authorities, the Athabasca Health Authority and the Saskatchewan Cancer Agency as well as a number of healthcare organizations. Over its large land base, approximately two-thirds of residents reside in urban regions.

The Challenge
Prior to 2010, each regional health authority in the province undertook strategic and operational planning independently, and did not contribute directly to the Ministry of Health's overarching health system plan. There was little alignment between the goals and actions of individual health regions and provincial priorities.

The Approach
In early 2010, Ministry leaders who were already using Lean for process improvement met with an American healthcare organization that utilizes a *Hoshin Kanri* approach to strategic planning. *Hoshin Kanri* is a methodology by which goals are determined, plans to achieve the goals are established, and measures are created to ensure progress toward identified goals. Attention and resources are applied system-wide in a disciplined, coordinated manner to accomplish large system goals. This was the first time Ministry leaders were exposed to *Hoshin Kanri* and they were intrigued by the process.

In the fall of 2011, health system leaders recognized the importance of building the internal capacity, infrastructure, and overall organizational culture to further advance Lean in Saskatchewan and decided to develop and deploy Lean as a management system (known as the Lean Management System). Saskatchewan was the first province in Canada to apply the Lean Management System across its entire health sector. Nearly twenty health organizations have now been part of deployment of Lean Management in the province's healthcare system.

The appeal of coordinating towards a collective focus was viewed as the suitable approach for Saskatchewan as a way to transform the sector into a patient-and family-centered system that thinks and acts as one. The Lean Management System provides a structured and disciplined approach to implementing improvements, both at a strategic level as well as at an

---

[4] http://www.stats.gov.sk.ca/

operational level. Through this process, the sector has shifted the way it undertakes health system planning to better identify and strategically prioritize work.

In 2011, a U.S.-based external Lean consultant was engaged and *Hoshin Kanri* was formally initiated. The approach taken was referred to as "teach, learn, do," which meant that the consultant fully supported and led the process for the first year, the Ministry led the process the second year with consultant support, and in the third year of implementation the Ministry led and fully supported the process. This approach worked well in terms of providing the knowledge and experience so that Ministry officials could take the process forward. It also allowed for Ministry ownership of the process, leading to discussion about how best to adjust the process to fit within a Saskatchewan context. In line with Lean thinking, the process itself continues to evolve and improve.

Through the *Hoshin Kanri* process, each of the aforementioned organizations now develops a strategic plan that aligns with the overarching plan into which they provided input. Further, through the Catchball process within *Hoshin Kanri*, experts in each organization are able to contribute to development of the plan. The plan therefore represents the perspective of the Ministry and the system, resulting in increased support for the plan and greater success achieving the goals within it. Lean and patient-and family-centered care have been foundational for achieving the health system's strategic goals: *Better Health, Better Care, Better Value, and Better Teams*.

The Results

Thanks to *Hoshin Kanri*, the Saskatchewan healthcare system is now a large coordinated system in which health regions collectively contribute to provincial direction and deliver health services accordingly.

Hoshin Kanri has also increased engagement within the health sector and improved the level of accountability expected for achieving results. This has occurred through the use of visibility walls which have been established at both provincial and organizational levels and have been cascaded to include frontline services, for example, hospital wards and emergency departments. Visibility walls contain the outcomes and targets, the health system's goals, as well as key projects and measures used to assess performance.

Hoshin Kanri has helped to assign responsibility to health system leaders for certain outcomes, projects, and measures. During wall walks (or reviews), each "owner" speaks to his or her area of responsibility and explains whether projects and goals are on target or not. If a project is not on target, leaders are expected to explain the problem that is occurring, as well as what action will be taken to correct it. Leaders, therefore, have direct responsibility for certain outcomes, projects, and targets and are held accountable by their peers during regular performance reviews.

While buy-in wasn't immediate among all leaders in the Ministry and the system, the evidence-informed rigor and coordinated structure of *Hoshin Kanri* was appealing. The *Hoshin Kanri* process relies upon an unprecedented level of involvement from both health system leaders as well as others within the system. Every year since its implementation, approximately forty-five health system leaders have been engaged in the development of the health system strategic plan. System leaders include CEOs and board chairs from twelve regional health authorities, Athabasca Health Authority, Saskatchewan Cancer Agency, Health Quality Council, eHealth Saskatchewan, 3sHealth, six physician representatives, and the Deputy Minister and Assistant Deputy Ministers of Health. In addition, a large number of middle management staff from these participating organizations are also engaged in the planning process.

This involvement and engagement has led to stronger teams and shared success as the system continually works to meet bold targets. Not only has engaging the sector been an innovative approach to strategic planning, it has brought alignment to the work. Today, in health facilities across the province, visibility walls are in place, which demonstrate that system partners are now focused on the same priorities, with clear alignment to overarching provincial goals.

The Future

Hoshin Kanri requires resources and effort to sustain momentum. Strong coordination and communication are critical to keeping the cycle on track. The accountability piece is challenging, especially when there is no formal authority over colleagues. Senior leaders in the Saskatchewan health-care system recognize that it will continue to be critical for them to endorse the work so it can progress effectively. In addition, while some employees have tried to use select Lean tools or pieces of the *Hoshin Kanri* process (that is, wall walks) and although that can work, leaders know that to achieve strategic and operational objectives, *Hoshin Kanri* is far more effective and is even more successful if it is undertaken and positioned within the larger Lean Management System.

With the success of *Hoshin Kanri* come other improvements in planning processes. Over time, Saskatchewan intends to more tightly weave together the elements of budget, planning, and reporting so that strategic planning, which is evidence-informed, will better inform the province's budget process. In January 2017, the provincial government also announced its intention to consolidate the twelve existing Regional Health Authorities. Launched in the fall of 2017, the Provincial Health Authority intends to continue its use of innovation and continuous improvement to transform service delivery across the continuum of healthcare.

Chapter 7

NUDGING WITH LEAN

In June 2014, the authors were introduced to the concept of Nudge theory for the first time. This theory is founded in the mechanics of behavior change and we were immediately struck by the potential to leverage the power of Nudge by using it in concert with Lean to improve public services. On its own, each approach has significant potential to make public services run more efficiently and effectively for both the organizations and the citizens they service. Combined, the possibilities seem endless – for policy design and implementation, the delivery of frontline services, and for streamlining back office processes.

By combining the best of Lean and Nudge theory, we believe there is broad and far-reaching potential to re-energize public services in the public interest. In fact, as our case studies show, we argue that some of the underlying principles of Nudge are already being used, unknowingly, and perhaps on an ad hoc basis, in Lean improvement projects around the world. What would happen if Nudge concepts and best practice were aligned with Lean methods in a structured and disciplined way?

The "What" and "Why" of Nudge

The origins of Nudge theory are rooted in the 1974 seminal work of Daniel Kahneman and Amos Tversky, two prominent cognitive psychologists who challenged the foundational beliefs of human decision-making and rationality. Through clever experimentation, Kahneman and Tversky were able to demonstrate that people tend to rely on "gut intuition" to drive their decision-making processes and behavior. This finding is in direct opposition to the popular notion that decision-making is founded in a rational and calculated expectation of utility or the weighing of pros and cons.

Relying on an intuitive process leads to "cognitive biases" in which normal human judgment systematically departs from being fully rational. Biases can cause people to misjudge important facts, be inconsistent in their perception of events and judgment of alternatives, miscalculate probabilities or the likelihood of an event occurring, be unconsciously influenced by the decisions of those around them, be sensitive to the way choices are framed and presented, prefer smaller but immediate rewards over larger delayed ones, and understand value in relative (rather than objective) terms.

In 2008, Richard Thaler and Cass Sunstein freed Nudge theory from its academic roots with the publication of the acclaimed book, *Nudge: Improving Decisions About Health, Wealth, and Happiness*. In this book, Thaler and Sunstein apply Khaneman and Tversky's cognitive theory to nudge people into making more rational (and less vulnerable) decisions.

It is important to note that proponents of applied Nudge theory believe, first and foremost, in free choice. They believe people should have good information, be free to make informed decisions, and be confident in their action as it relates to their decision-making process (Thaler and Sunstein, 2008). They do recognize, however, that sometimes the required information is not available or is too complex for a non-expert to comprehend and in this instance, rational actions can be encouraged through defaults, decision aids, and the careful design of choice architecture (Kahneman, 2013).

Nudge theory advocates the design of choices for people to encourage positive decision-making for the individual and, ideally, for society as a whole. It supports actively influencing and encouraging people to make decisions through a stable and relevant thought process that is beneficial for the person and society as a whole. It also recognizes that people often fail to take the necessary action to opt in to or opt out of programs and services, or make decisions that could be helpful for them or others. Therefore, it supports the creation of default options so that, in the absence of decision, individuals will be "nudged" in a direction consistent with their best interests (Thaler and Sunstein, 2008).

The theory has proven especially useful in the public sector. Governments in the UK, U.S., and Canada, to name a few, are creating specialized "Nudge Units" to apply the insights from behavioral economics to tweak traditional and/or existing policies, test the impact, and roll out implementations with the goal of shifting societal behaviors. In 2014, Canada established a central Innovation Hub in the Privy Council Office in part to support behavioral or "nudge" economics. The Organisation for Economic Development and Co-operation (OECD) has also explored the role of behavioral economics in consumer decision-making and has published a *Consumer Policy Toolkit* (2010) to help government policymakers worldwide decide when to intervene in a market to address a consumer problem. In 2015 the World Bank set up a group that is applying behavioral economics in fifty-two poor countries and the UN is now using nudge to hit its sustainable development goals (*The Economist*, May 20, 2017).

Some examples of large-scale uses of Nudge theory include:

- By 2015, automatic enrollment in pensions upon commencement of employment, rather than the traditional "opting in" requirement via an application process, led to more than five million extra UK workers saving for their pensions (Halpern, 2015);
- Randomized control trials conducted in the UK in 2013 indicate that changing the language used to ask people to become organ donors to, "If you needed an organ transplant, would you have one?" will result in more than one hundred thousand more people a year carrying donor cards (Halpern, 2015);
- Also in the UK, letters sent to people who were not paying their vehicle tax were simplified along the line of "pay your tax or lose your car." This resulted in twice as many people paying their tax. Some people also received a photograph of their car with the letter. This tripled the number of people who paid (*The Economist*, 2012);
- It was discovered in the UK that homeowners were not applying for an insulation grant to make their homes more energy efficient because they would have to go through the process of clearing out their attic. A Nudge was put in place whereby insulation firms would offer to clear the attic, get rid of unwanted items, and return the items to be kept after insulating. This resulted in a 30 to 45 percent increase in take-up of the grant (Halpern, 2015);
- Nudge practices such as requirements for information disclosure, consumer warnings, and default rules have been incorporated into many

U.S. and UK initiatives involving energy efficiency, fuel economy, environmental protection, smoking cessation, charitable donation, consumer protection, and obesity (Sunstein, *Why Nudge?* 2014).

Nudge is seen as a tool for government – as an additional lens to traditional policy development tools such as legislation, regulation, or taxation and a means for making government smaller and more modest. Nudge theory advocates maximizing choice for the public through information, transparency, participation, collaboration, and simplification (Sunstein, 2010). This is where Lean comes in. We believe it is the ideal methodology for incorporating Nudge theory in a deliberate way to achieve, renew, and transform policies, programs, and processes. By *Nudging with Lean*, governments, at all levels, can maximize choice for citizens in accordance with the public interest.

Lean Methods and Nudge Practices

When public-sector organizations use Lean methods or apply Nudge theory, they do so because they want to create better, safer, and more efficient services. They are seeking to improve outcomes for the most valued stakeholders – citizens, clients, customers, and employees – and ultimately, get better return on investment/value for money for taxpayers.

In Chapter 1, we described a variety of Lean methods and, throughout this book we have used case studies to illustrate their use in public-sector organizations across Canada. Now, we will demonstrate the alignment between the Lean and Nudge methodologies and show they can be adapted to incorporate the application of Nudge practices to improve public service outcomes.

Libertarian Paternalism, Choice Architecture, and Lean

A key concept of Nudge is "libertarian paternalism" which advocates freedom of choice while recognizing as legitimate the design of policies, programs, and services so as to influence people's behavior in ways that will make life longer, healthier, and better. Such "choice architecture" is required because "individuals make pretty bad decisions – decisions they would not have made if they had paid full attention and possessed complete information, unlimited cognitive abilities and complete self-control" (Thaler and Sunstein, 2008, p.5).

What if the notion of libertarian paternalism was incorporated into

Lean methods and processes? After all, the individuals involved in these Lean events are the choice architects. They are actively engaged in reviewing policies and procedures to achieve improved outcomes and reach an optimal target or goal. They are the clients, customers, managers, and employees involved in the "real work" of service delivery. They understand the business from the perspective of customer and provider, and are in a perfect position to consider what nudges may be introduced along the value stream to improve decision-making by customers and service providers.

Every Lean event puts the client or customer at the forefront and challenges the people who are engaged to simplify processes, reduce waste, and redirect resources to achieve better service and enhanced efficiency. By introducing questions such as "how can we help our stakeholders make better choices for themselves and the business?" "how can we provide better and more clear information to ensure stakeholders are informed?" "how can we encourage people to think and act in accordance with their long-term best interests?" and "how can we change the work environment so employees spend more time with the client?" we can *Nudge with Lean*.

Lean Is a Nudge

We also believe that many Lean methods are, in and of themselves, nudges. Lean, by its very nature, makes problems transparent and promotes the design of solutions accordingly. Often, these are nudges designed to impact the behaviors of citizens and/or employees.

Disciplined strategic management and deployment (*Hoshin Kanri*), for example, nudges leaders to prioritize, focus, and "think and act as one" to achieve improvement. Lean tools such as A3s, continuous improvement plans and corrective action plans enable organizations to "plan, do, check, and adjust," thereby nudging improvement. Visual displays and wall walks nudge through continuous reinforcement of progress and accountability (or the lack of it). 5S nudges employee productivity by decluttering and maintaining safe, orderly work spaces.

Lean Management tools such as daily huddles, the *Gemba*, and leader standard work are intended to ensure "line of sight" for all employees so they understand their role in the fulfillment of organizational goals and objectives. Lean Management is about nudging employee output, engagement, problem solving, innovation, and commitment to the organization – all of which are necessary to achieving improved outcomes in service, safety, and efficiency.

> **CASE STUDY**
> **Visual Management and Productivity, British Columbia Crown Corporation**
>
> **The Challenge**
> A major crown corporation in BC had significant backlogs and was unable to serve customers on a timely basis. Significant complaints were being received from frustrated customers, and employees were disengaged.
>
> **The Strategy and Results:**
> The corporation decided to use Lean Management to better engage employees to improve the efficiency of operations. One tool used was the development of a visual wall to capture and display metrics about daily volumes and backlogs. The content of the wall was reviewed daily by management and employees so everyone was aware of volumes and engaged in generating solutions.
>
> Employees typically had worked for the corporation for many years (20+) and were accustomed to doing things the way they had always done them. Initially, they were wary of change and suspicious about management's agenda. Two weeks following establishment of the visual wall, two unionized employees demanded it be removed. Management complied.
>
> Three to four days later, other employees requested the wall be reinstated because they recognized it helped them to better understand volumes, and that they liked being part of solution-finding aimed at improving the customer experience. The visual wall was re-established.
>
> Fifteen weeks later, the service backlog had been eliminated and productivity had increased by 20 percent. Use of the visual wall had *nudged* long-term employees into being part of the solution to increasing customer service by increasing productivity.

Nudging with Lean

To positively influence outcomes, we propose introducing a variety of Nudge practices directly in Lean events. By using Lean and Nudge, and by *Nudging with Lean*, we can transform public services to better meet the needs and expectations of clients and customers. People are at the heart of improvement and innovation and by bringing them together, innovative solutions can be found to complex problems resulting in better, safer, and fiscally prudent public services. This benefits all of us, as is aptly described in the following case study by the City of Denver's Brian Elms and J.B.Wogan.

CASE STUDY
The City of Denver, Colorado
The Gift of Time by Brian Elms and J.B.Wogan

I don't think a day goes by that I don't hear someone complaining about waiting in line at a government agency. In fact, over the weekend I was at one of Denver's popular brew pubs and overheard three guys complaining about getting their license plates renewed. I just started chuckling at them, when one of them said: "You feel me!" When I responded "no," they looked perplexed.

About 240,000 people use the Denver DMV to renew their license plates each year. Of those 240,000, how many would you think use our website to perform their renewal transactions? If you said 50 percent, I would have believed you. That is exactly what I thought. However, a mere 34 percent use our website. Another 30 percent mail us a physical check. That means the three guys complaining are among the 86,000 people who still come into the DMV for a simple transaction.

For more than four years, the Denver Peak team has provided training and support to all city departments including the DMV or Department of Motor Vehicles. The team is charged with increasing the capacity of the City and County of Denver by teaching process improvement skills like Lean to our more than thirteen thousand employees. To date, they have trained more than 5,500 employees in four years. www.denverpeak.com

We are constantly looking for new techniques and ideas to test in our incredible laboratory, the City and County of Denver. And, as a continuous improvement convert, I am always looking for new sources of inspiration, which is how I ended up listening to the audio book of *Nudge* by Cass Sunstein and Richard Thaler. Their argument is simple: humans make decisions every day based on how information is provided to them. If you provide information in the right way, humans will make the right decision. Sunstein and Thaler also introduced me to the concept of "libertarian paternalism." This means that you don't remove all the choices, you continue to offer them, but attempt to focus people's attention on the one you think will benefit them over time.

The book resonated with my team because it identified some ideas we already practice under another name. For example, we "nudge" people to avoid errors through a Lean technique called mistake-proofing. Ever since reading *Nudge*, we've wanted to incorporate more of its lessons in our own work. Not long after we started implementing Nudge techniques on our own, and as luck would have it, we received a grant from Bloomberg Philanthropies to receive technical assistance on Nudge interventions through the foundation's What Works Cities initiative. The Behavior Insights Team, experts on Nudge techniques after years of experience using them for government programs in the United Kingdom, flew to Denver and trained the Peak team. Their instructors, Elspeth Kirkman and Lis Costa, broke down just how we can tap into the world of behavior economics and choice architecture with simple and easy-to-use playing cards. http://www.behaviouralinsights.co.uk/publications/east-four-simple-ways-to-apply-behavioural-insights/

So, we went for it. How can the City and County of Denver get 85,997 people to stay at home and perform the transaction online rather than coming in to the DMV? We pulled around twenty employees together and worked through the Behavior Insights Team techniques to come up with some marketing messages on a postcard that we would send out in a randomized control trial to see if our instincts actually worked.

Checklist Postcard (Front)

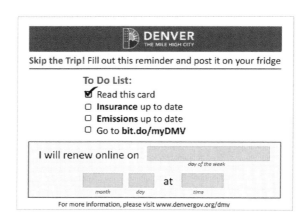

DELIVERING RESULTS THAT MATTER

Checklist Postcard (Back)

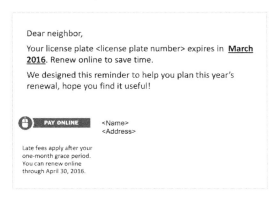

The two postcards use two different human behaviors. The first postcard uses a checklist and a commitment strategy. The second postcard uses another strategy based on the assumption that humans like to plan. Each postcard saw an increase in online usage. The postcard using a checklist saw an increase of 6.8 percent and the postcard using planning saw a 7.8 percent increase. Combined, if we choose to run this at full scale and not just a randomized control trial, we could see up to nine thousand fewer people using the physical counter at the DMV to renew their license plates.

I get it. It isn't eighty thousand, but it is a major dent, and even with nine thousand fewer in-person visitors, we could see incredible reduction in wait times at the DMV. For more than four years, our directors at the DMV have focused on wait-time reductions. I am pleased to let you know that over the last few years, our wait time averages have gone from one hour and thirty minutes to what they are today: around twenty minutes! This is the next technique we will deploy to continue to look for ways our teams can reduce the customer's time in a transaction with the government. Our hope is that one day there is less wait and tons of value, just like what is provided by Amazon or Zappos.

In 2016, our team completed more than seven different behavior insights or Nudges. We use this technique all over the place now in Denver. We are using it with the Elections team to get voters to turn in ballots earlier. We are using the technique to help reduce the residents of Denver that receive Bench Warrants or even reduce the amount of parking tickets we issue on game day for the Denver Broncos.

These techniques prescribed in *Nudge* and taught by the Behavior Insights Team are easy to use and make so much sense in the world of providing additional value to the customer. As we say in Peak, the greatest gift you can give the residents is their time.

Chapter 8

INTEGRATING LEAN MANAGEMENT WITH PUBLIC SECTOR DIGITAL TRANSFORMATION

Digital transformation is underway globally across business and industry and, while it is occurring in the public sector, it is lagging significantly behind private business. With increased demand from citizens and customers for faster and better access to services, including those available on personal mobile devices, business and government leaders are under immense pressure to improve business processes and digitize essential functions and services within their organizations. In order to successfully transform and become true digital enterprises, organizations need to engage citizens, customers, suppliers, partners, and employees in a thoughtful and disciplined manner. They must also leverage the appropriate digital technologies to improve customer experiences and better address customer needs. Organizations stand to gain more value from their digital investment if they develop and manage integrated computer systems, often referred to as enterprise resource planning (ERP). As they do so, it will be advantageous to use Lean thinking to integrate process improvement with digital experience and technology.

As discussed in earlier chapters, there is a common perception among many senior managers and technology leaders that Lean is only about process improvement. Lean is viewed as something that frontline staff use to fix processes to address day-to-day operational challenges that have very little to do with management. The concept of Lean Management as a system that can change organizational culture by adjusting how managers manage and how staff think and behave in the workplace eludes most business and technology leaders. Technology leaders, IT consultants, and implementers of ERP systems often do not value the potential of Lean thinking to effectively implement technology systems aimed at improving frontline services which impact the customer, or back end internally focused application systems. ERP systems are often viewed as a panacea for all of the operational weakness in the organization. However, ERP systems are effective only when the entire business process is "baked" into the system and, unfortunately, this is rarely the case. End-to-end process improvement may impact multiple organizational functions and departments, multiple IT systems, and most of the staff within an organization. If not executed effectively, there will be waste, errors, as well as a proliferation of low or non-valued work. Even more troubling is that ERP implementations generally don't include new ways of thinking and working that promote accountability, measurement, and drive for continuous improvement in organizations.

Digital Experience and Lean Management share a powerful common principle: *provide exactly what the customers (internal and external) need, when they need it, in the quantity they need, in the right sequence, without defects, and at the lowest possible cost.* Integrating the Lean Management philosophy in organizations' digital transformation journeys can benefit these institutions in many ways. It can deliver increased value to customers, reduce delivery time of digital services, realize early cost savings and capacity gains and, most importantly, change the way people think, feel, and behave in the workplace.

Integration of Lean Management

While the rewards of technology-driven transformations can be considerable, the risks of these projects are also significant given the strategic imperative, cost, and number of resources involved. The frequency of failure is high, with recent studies finding that 75 percent of technology transformation initiatives fail to fulfill their stated goals and objectives (Mark J. Dawson and Mark L. Jones 2007), (Willis Towers Watson, 2013). Since the early 2000s we have consistently seen three reasons for project failure:

- Changes in scope mid-project
- Poor estimates during the planning phase

- Insufficient resources

In our experience, many technology-driven transformations also fail to solve the "right" business problems. Requirement gathering activities can be focused on simply asking users what they want. This may result in automating ineffective processes and lead to minimal improvement. In some cases, users may find the new processes even more frustrating. Improvements left on the table mean that new technology is not being fully leveraged and the return on investment is low.

The concept of improving process before technology is not a new one. Indeed, many organizations have learned to adapt their approach to technology transformation based on lessons learned. But improving business processes is often seen as a separate activity from technology implementation. What if we were to fully integrate Lean Management, customer experience, and technology implementation into one overall transformation methodology? The strengths of each approach can be very effective in offsetting the limitations of the other strategies. One of the most effective Lean Management tools to identify the right business problems and to develop a strategic roadmap for improvement is "Value Stream Mapping."

Value Stream Mapping (VSM) is a Lean tool used to map all the current end-to-end steps taken to deliver something of value to a customer as well as providing a vision of a future state process. A VSM improvement event is meant to cut across departments and handoffs within an organization. Customers experience processes end-to-end and they are generally not concerned with a company's organizational structure and internal silos. During a VSM event, typically attended by frontline process workers representing multiple functions, Lean practitioners focus on applying the core Lean principles (eliminating wasteful steps and introducing flow and pull to a process). If we involve user experience and technology professionals as full participants in a VSM event, the result can be truly remarkable. User experience professionals can provide valuable input to the customers' experience of a process. Technology professionals can recommend the right functionality to solve pressing business problems. The result is a shared vision of process changes that is complemented by appropriate technology changes. In the Lean world, this becomes a "Continuous Improvement Plan" (CIP) that lays out required process changes along with a plan and timelines for implementing these changes. In the software world, this becomes a "Technology Road Map" that lays out the development plan.

This vision addresses common issues by redefining the appropriate project scope by removing unnecessary or redundant processes before they need to be coded, providing a better understanding of the resourcing requirements across all work streams, and creating a flexible implementation plan to manage risks associated with estimating. This type of strategic roadmap is ideally suited to an "Agile" implementation approach. Agile is an industry standard term which refers to a method of incremental software development rather than a traditional "waterfall" approach where an entire IT system is developed and then implemented at the same time. Agile focuses on iterative development and incremental improvement with a relentless focus on value for prioritization. Each "sprint" delivers working, tested software or processes for immediate feedback from users. This is a more adaptive method and can be a significant improvement over the more traditional waterfall method.

Some improvement events can be pure process changes that are independent of technology. Others may be dependent on technology and may require more detailed requirement gathering sessions. Change becomes a series of incremental improvements rather than a big bang. Customers can have more precise working software and process changes within weeks instead of years. Organizations can get a faster return on technology investment and are better able to accommodate customer feedback.

Figure 8-1 Lean Management Techniques lists some of the most commonly used Lean Management practices, described more fully in earlier chapters, that can significantly improve the accuracy of technology requirements, create staff engagement, dramatically increase ROI, and provide an opportunity to implement new work behaviors that promote a culture of continuous improvement. A case study then follows to illustrate integrated Lean Management with public sector digital transformation.

Figure 8-1 Lean Management Techniques

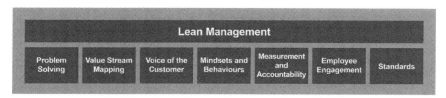

The work plan in Figure 8-2 below illustrates what a high-level timeline of integrating Lean Management, Digital Experience, and Technology might look like.

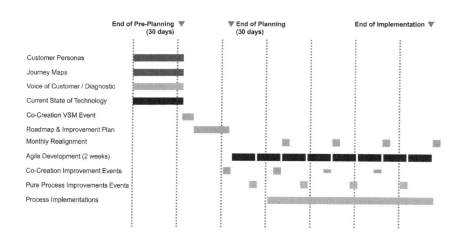

Figure 8-2 Sample Integrated Lean/Digital/IT Work Plan

CASE STUDY
Financial Services Organization

The Challenge

A large public sector financial services organization (a Canadian crown corporation) was challenged by lack of functionality and user-friendliness of its online presence. Its online capabilities were limited from a customer experience and functionality perspective. This, in turn, led to poor staff productivity.

The Approach

To better serve its customers, the organization embarked on a major technology transformation initiative using cutting edge client relationship management software developed by Salesforce, an American cloud computing company. The organization combined Agile delivery with Lean Management to harness the benefits of both approaches and ensure successful implementation. This entailed behavior change among management and staff as well as the measurement and tracking of value-added benefits at the program and enterprise level.

The Results

By integrating technology and Lean Management with Agile delivery, the organization has been able to implement efficient and effective business processes and prototype technology changes to support its digital transformation. Agile delivery combined with Value Stream Mapping has made it possible for employees to identify and address risks early. It has also provided leaders with better insight into what customers and staff are demanding in terms of IT functionality.

In the first three months of implementation through a series of six VSM events, the process improvement team identified nearly four million dollars in efficiencies and provided a number of detailed process changes and opportunities for the technology team. The technology team was able to rapidly design, develop, and deliver a functional customer and staff portal that fixed the most pressing problem identified by the staff _ the inability to see all customer information in one place.

The organization's leadership and employees across all product lines created new processes that fully utilize modern technology. The combined Lean Management and Agile delivery approach improved quality, reduced cycle time for product delivery, and built internal capacity for the organization to take on future improvement initiatives.

As an added benefit, the organization was able to develop its internal capability in Lean Management by completing Lean Yellow belt training,

> Lean Leadership training, and development of an internal Operational Excellence team. A "See-Learn-Do" approach was used to help develop internal staff. Training and coaching provided by external consultants helped individuals within the organization learn to apply fundamental Lean Management tools, principles, and techniques applicable to the knowledge environment throughout the organization.

Conclusion

The U.S. National Institutes of Health, the Insurance Corporation of British Columbia, Lower Mainland Facilities Management, Export Development Canada, the City of Denver, Washington State, and the Government of Saskatchewan, all profiled in this book, are public sector Lean leaders. What do they have in common? They have strong leadership that is committed to continuously improving programs and services for the benefit of their customers. We hope their experience and the practical advice provided in this book will inspire you to embark on your own Lean journey or, if you have already begun, help you to move forward to integrate and sustain the approach across your organization.

This book is based on our direct experience in implementing Lean thinking corporate-wide at a number of government and public-sector organizations over the last fifteen years. Governments and the citizens they serve will benefit greatly if Lean thinking is instilled in a structured and planned manner through ongoing training and hands-on involvement of frontline staff and managers at all levels. Results will follow if there is strong leadership commitment, accountability, and daily performance management through grassroots engagement and involvement.

We encourage you to familiarize yourself with the Lean concepts and techniques covered in Chapter 1, think about who your customers are, and ask them what they need and expect from your organization (Chapter 2). Whether you have already begun your Lean journey or are just beginning, as Chapter 3 describes, you can expect to go through several phases over several years before Lean is fully embedded in the culture of your organization. Implementing Lean is challenging and, above all, it requires strong, committed leadership, and disciplined management (Chapter 4). It will also necessitate leaders and managers to change the way they manage to more directly involve and empower frontline employees to solve problems and continuously improve – this is the only way the improvements can be sustained. As you continue with your Lean journey you will likely want to be more strategic and use Lean thinking to address complex issues as the case study on Results Washington describes in Chapter 5. You may also consider using a more structured approach to strategic planning and deployment to ensure organizational plans are implemented, adapted, and improved over time (Chapter 6). Finally, as Lean becomes fully integrated within your organization you may wish to combine it with other approaches such as Nudge (Chapter 7) and with your digital and information technology strategies (Chapter 8).

Public sector Lean implementation is alive and flourishing across the world with many national, state, provincial, and municipal governments as well as government-funded agencies such as school divisions, colleges and, in some countries, the health sector using Lean to lead manage and improve public services. There is an increasing awareness that Lean is about more than just process improvement and that it can, in fact, be used to accomplish transformational change within an organization. Through disciplined application, leaders can use Lean to deliver on strategic objectives and they can work horizontally to tackle significant challenges. In addition, they can lever the expertise of their workforce and engage citizens and the users of public services in improvement efforts while simultaneously building a culture of integrity and respect within their organization.

In our experience, public employees from the executive level to the frontline are committed to making things better for the people who access programs and services as well as for the taxpayers who pay for them. They want to deliver results that matter to the governments they serve and, ultimately, to the people. As you move forward on your Lean journey, we wish you well and would appreciate hearing from you about your accomplishments and challenges. Please tell us your story by emailing whiteshell@sasktel.net and haneef.chagani@gmail.com.

Bibliography

CBC News, Saskatchewan, Canada. "More Grade 3 kids reading at grade level, Sask. government says," Oct. 28, 2016. http://www.cbc.ca/news/canada/saskatchewan/grade-3-reading-level-sask-1.3826320

Chagani, Haneef, "Achieving Operational Excellence through Lean Transformation: Introduction to Lean," PricewaterhouseCoopers LLP, Oct. 29, 2014, http://ppx.ca/wp-content/uploads/2015/08/Introduction_to_Lean_PPX_Conference_Oct_2014.pdf.

Dawson, Mark J., and Mark L. Jones, "Human Change Management: Herding Cats," PwC, 2007.

Dennis, Patrick. *Getting the Right Things Done: A Leader's Guide to Planning and Execution*. Cambridge, MA: Lean Enterprise Institute, 2006.

Elms, Brian, and J.B. Wogan. *Peak Performance: How Denver's Peak Academy is Saving Money, Boosting Morale and Just Maybe Changing the World. (And How You Can, Too!)*. Washington, DC: Governing Books, 2016.

"Free exchange: Nudge nudge, think think," *The Economist*, Mar. 24, 2012, http://www.economist.com/node/21551032.

Get Lean Florida (website), State of Florida, http://getleanflorida.com/.

Government of Saskatchewan, Conference Presentation Organized by Johnson Shoyama Graduate School of Public Policy, July 2016.

Halpern, David. *Inside the Nudge Unit: How Small Changes Can Make a Big Difference*. London: Ebury Press, 2016.

International Association for Public Participation, "Public Participation Spectrum," http://iap2canada.ca/page-1020549.

Kahneman, Daniel. *Thinking, Fast and Slow*. New York: Farrar, Straus and Giroux, 2013.

Lean Enterprise Institute, "What is Lean? > Principles," https://www.lean.org/WhatsLean/Principles.cfm.

LeanOhio (website), Ohio Department of Administrative Services, http://www.lean.ohio.gov/.

"Making government work: When nudge comes to shove," *The Economist*, May 20, 2017, 59-60.

Mann, David. *Creating a Lean Culture: Tools to Sustain Lean Conversions, Second Edition*. New York: Productivity Press, 2010.

Minnesota Office of Continuous Improvement! (website), Minnesota Department of Administration/Continuous Improvement, https://mn.gov/admin/continuous-improvement/.

OECD, "Consumer Policy Toolkit," July 9, 2010, http://www.oecd.org/sti/consumer/consumer-policy-toolkit-9789264079663-en.htm.

Provincial Auditor of Saskatchewan, "2015 Report Volume 2," Dec. 8, 2015, https://auditor.sk.ca/publications/public-reports/item?id=140.

Results Iowa (website), State of Iowa, http://www.resultsiowa.org/.

Results Washington (website), State of Washington, http://www.results.wa.gov/.

Smith, Dick, and Jerry Blakeslee. *Strategic Six Sigma: Best Practices from the Executive Suite*. Hoboken, NJ: John Wiley & Sons, Inc., 2002.

Sunstein, Cass R., "Memorandum for the Heads of Executive Departments and Agencies: Disclosure and Simplification as Regulatory Tools," Office of Management and Budget, June 18, 2010, https://obamawhitehouse.archives.gov/sites/default/files/omb/assets/inforeg/disclosure_principles.pdf.

Sunstein, Cass R. *Why Nudge? The Politics of Libertarian Paternalism*. New Haven, CT: Yale University Press, 2014.

Teeuwen, Bert. *Lean for the Public Sector: The Pursuit of Perfection in Government Services.* New York: Productivity Press, 2010.

Thaler, Richard H., and Cass R. Sunstein. *Nudge: Improving Decisions About Health, Wealth, and Happiness.* New Haven, CT: Yale University Press, 2008.

U.S. Environmental Protection Agency, "Lean Government Methods Guide," June 2013, https://www.epa.gov/sites/production/files/2014-01/documents/lean-methods-guide.pdf.

Washburn, Jane, "Pursuing Excellence in the Government of New Brunswick," *ASQC, Government Division* 17, no. 2 (Summer 2014), 1-3.

Washington State Correctional Industries, "Our Mandate," August 2014.

Washington State Correctional Industries, "Planting the Seed of Change," August 2013, https://www.washingtonci.com/skin/frontend/WACI/primary/docs/content/about-ci/who-we-are/sustainability/sustainability-brochure.pdf.

Washington State Department of Corrections, "2017-2021 Strategic Plan," http://www.doc.wa.gov/docs/publications//100-SP001.pdf.

Washington State Department of Corrections, "Correctional Industries (CI)," http://www.doc.wa.gov/corrections/programs/correctional-industries.htm.

Washington State Institute for Public Policy, "Return on Investment: Evidence-Based Options to Improve Statewide Outcomes," April 2012, http://www.wsipp.wa.gov/ReportFile/1102/Wsipp_Return-on-Investment-Evidence-Based-Options-to-Improve-Statewide-Outcomes-April-2012-Update_Full-Report.pdf.

Washington State Institute for Public Policy, "Washington's Residential Drug Offender Sentencing Alternative: *Recidivism & Cost Analysis,*" Dec. 2014, http://www.wsipp.wa.gov/ReportFile/1577/Wsipp_Washingtons-Residential-Drug-Offender-Sentencing-Alternative-Recidivism-Cost-Analysis_Report.pdf.

Willis Towers Watson, "2013-2014 Change and Communication ROI Study: The 10th Anniversary Report," Dec. 2013, https://www.

towerswatson.com/en-US/Insights/IC-Types/Survey-Research-Results/2013/12/2013-2014-change-and-communication-roi-study.

Womack, James P., and Daniel T. Jones. *Lean Thinking: Banish Waste and Create Wealth in Your Corporation*. New York: Productivity Press, 1996.

About the Authors

We are privileged to have been directly involved in public sector Lean implementation. We've seen the benefits as well as the challenges of managing complex change in public service environments. We believe the potential to expand use of Lean across the public sector is enormous; we hope this book will provide an effective way to spread the word. We draw on our experience and use real-life case examples and case studies to illustrate why we are so committed to Lean.

Haneef Chagani is a management consultant specializing in assisting organizations to develop efficient and effective business operations. He has more than twenty years' experience in helping clients transform their businesses to attain higher levels of performance. He has assisted organizations improve customer service, reduce millions of dollars in costs, create new capacity, and increase productivity by improving core processes and driving culture change throughout the organization.

Haneef has trained and coached thousands of Lean Six Sigma practitioners, program champions, and senior executives in Operational Excellence philosophies, methodology, tools and techniques. Haneef was a Partner at PricewaterhouseCoopers, LLP and led the firm's Operational Excellence practice in Canada.

Haneef holds an MBA from Simon Fraser University and a BSc. in Computer Science from the University of Manchester, UK. He is a certified Management Consultant and a Lean Six Sigma Master Black Belt and lives in Burnaby, British Columbia, Canada.

Shelley Whitehead is a writer, researcher, and social policy consultant with White Shell Resources. She worked for the Government of Saskatchewan for thirty-four years. For seven years, she provided advice, support, and oversight for enterprise projects including Lean implementation across the provincial government, school divisions, and post-secondary institutions. She also served as Assistant Deputy Minister, Policy with the Ministry of Social Services and has worked in a variety of central agencies and direct delivery ministries. Shelley has spoken extensively on public sector Lean implementation across Canada and has facilitated a variety of policy workshops for graduate students in public policy. She began her career as a frontline social worker and has a BA from the University of Regina, a BSW from the University of Calgary, and an MSW from the University of Regina. She resides in Regina, Saskatchewan, Canada.

INDEX

B
Blucher, Mark, i
British Columbia, xx, 1, 35, 47, 53, 76, 81, 108, 119

C
Canada, xix-xx, 1, 24, 35, 50, 76, 81, 90, 100, 104-106, 119
Case Studies
   5S in a Canadian Highways Ministry, 12
   A Canadian Medical Laboratory, 8
   A Canadian Province's Ministry of Transportation, xx, 64
   Claims Front End Process Improvement, 10
   Export Development Canada (EDC), xx, 90-93, 119
   Financial Services Organization, xxi, 117
   Government of Saskatchewan, 1, 16-17, 50, 52, 119
   Insurance Corporation of British Columbia (ICBC), xx, 76, 119
   Lower Mainland Facilities Management, 81, 119
   Mistake Proofing in a Hospital, 9
   National Institutes of Health (NIH), 40-44
   New Canadian Regional Hospital, 14
   Oil and Gas Technical Application, 7
   Results Washington, xiv, xx, 2, 57-58, 63, 85-87, 120
   The City of Denver, Colorado, 109
   Using Hoshin Kanri Across Saskatchewan's Education Sector, 16
   Visual Management and Productivity, 108
   Washington State Correctional Industries, 25, 58
   Washington State Department of Corrections, xix-xx, 25, 57-59
Citizen and Government Roles, 23
Continuous Improvement Plan (CIP), 35-36, 48, 55, 61, 107, 114
Correctional industries (CI), 25-29, 58-59

D
Daily accountability, 68, 70
Deployment Trajectories, 38
Digital transformation, xxi, 112-113, 115, 117
DMAIC, 9-10, 41

INDEX

E
Economic Development and Co-operation (OECD), 90, 105
EDC Way, 91, 93
enterprise resource planning (ERP), 112-113
Export Development Canada (EDC), xx, 90-91, 93, 119

G
Governance, xix, 32, 45-47, 49, 54
Greenleaf, Robert K., 73

H
Harris, Mike, i, xii
Hoshin Kanri for strategic planning and deployment, 37
Hoshin Kanri plan, 16, 95, 98

I
Information Centers (IC), 28, 67, 77-78, 81, 95
Inslee, Jay, xiii, 85
Insurance Corporation of British Columbia (ICBC), xx, 76, 119
Inventory Metrics Reporting, 44

L
Lab Grade (LG) Freezer Accountability Project, 44
Leader Standard Work, 68-69, 71, 107
Leadership Behaviors, 18, 37-38, 68, 72
Leadership Discipline, 68, 71
Lean Deployment Champions, 35, 47, 50, 54
Lean Enterprise Institute, 4
Lean Journey
    Initiation, xix, 35, 41, 81, 85
    Integration, xix, 37, 41, 113
    Mobilization, xix, 33-34, 40
    Strategy and Assessment, 31, 40
    Sustainment, xix, 37, 42, 56
Lean Leader training, 36, 50, 53
Lean Leaders, xxi, 33, 35-37, 47-48, 54, 73, 75, 119
Lean leadership, 38, 66, 73-74, 118
Lean Management System, 68, 71, 74-75, 81, 100, 102
Lean mantra, 34, 73
Lean Maturity Assessment, 90
Lean Methods, xix, 4, 6, 25, 34-36, 46, 103, 106-107
Lean Office, 47, 50, 54, 56
Lean Principles, xiii-xiv, 4, 49, 85, 114
Lean Six Sigma, 9-10, 40, 42, 48
Lean Steering Committee, 47
Lean strategic planning, 94-95, 100
Lean thinking, xiii, xx, 2-4, 49, 58, 76, 83, 85, 91, 101, 112-113, 119-120

M
Measuring Lean Implementation, 60
Ministry of Highways Employee Testimonials, 12
Mistake Proofing, 8-9

INDEX

N

National Institutes of Health (NIH), 40-44
NIH Measurable Results, 43
Nudge theory, xx, 103-106
Nudging with Lean, 103, 106, 108

P

Plan-Do-Check-Adjust (PDCA), 72, 78, 99
Principal Elements of Lean Management, 67, 74
problem-solving technique, 67, 72, 77
Production, Preparation Process (3P), 13-14, 21
Public sector Lean implementation, xviii-xix, 1, 50, 120

R

Rapid Process Improvement Workshops (RPI), 7
Reporting Progress and Communicating Results, 61
Request for Proposals (RFP), 50, 54
Resource Allocation, 54
Rodent Cage Handling Process, 44

S

Saskatchewan, xx, 1-2, 16-17, 21, 25, 35, 50-55, 60, 100-102, 119
servant leadership, 73
states in the U.S
    Arizona, 1
    Colorado, 1, 109
    Connecticut, 1
    Iowa, 1, 63
    Minnesota, 1, 63
    Ohio, 1, 63
    Rhode Island, 1
    Tennessee, 1
    Wisconsin, 1
Sunstein, Cass, 104, 109
Supply Center Replenishment Process, 44
Sustained Lean Enterprise, 38

T

Teeuwen, Bert, 22
Thaler, Richard, 104, 109
Traditional Leadership, 72-73

U

Using Lean Strategic Planning and Deployment (Hoshin Kanri), xx, 15-16, 37, 94-102, 107

V

Value Stream Mapping (VSMs), 6-7, 21, 77-78, 81, 114, 117
Vancouver General Hospital, 81
Visibility Wall, 48, 67, 74, 95-99, 101-102
Visual Controls, 15, 67-71

W

Wall Walk, 96-99, 101-102, 107
Washington, xiii-xv, xix-xx, 1-2, 25, 28, 32, 48, 57-59, 63, 85-89, 119-120
waste in organizations
    Movement/Motion, 6
    Overprocessing, 5

INDEX

Overproduction, 5
Queues/Inventory, 6
Rework/Defects, 5
Transportation, 6
Underutilized people, 6
Waiting Time, 6
What Is Lean, 2, 66

Made in the USA
Columbia, SC
29 January 2018